CHRIS ALEXANDER'S
BLOOD SPATTERED BOOK

A Selection of Personal Essays on Underrated Horror, Dark Fantasy and Cult Movies that Refuse to Behave

Midnight Marquee Press, Inc.
Baltimore, Maryland, USA

Copyright © 2010 by Chris Alexander Filmwords
Interior and Cover Design: Susan Svehla

Without limiting the rights under copyright reserved above, no part of this publication may be reproduced, stored in or introduced into a retrieval system, or transmitted, in any form, or by any means (electronic, mechanical, photocopying, recording or otherwise), without the prior written permission of the copyright owner or the publishers of the book.

ISBN 13: 978-1936168-00-2
ISBN 10: 1-936168-00-6
Library of Congress Catalog Card Number 2009914226
Manufactured in the United States of America
First Printing by Midnight Marquee Press, Inc., Janurary 2010

Chris Alexander is able to swerve in and out of thoughts and images like traveling through a melody. His capacity to intuitively grasp the essence of an artist or film is strong and daring. Because of this, his subjects can be seen under a light otherwise kept in darkness.
—Coralina Cataldi-Tassoni, actress (Dario Argento's *Opera* and *Mother of Tears*) and musician

Dedication

For my little lads Jack and Elliot—
may they grow to love these strange slices of cinema
as much as their old man does…

CONTENTS

6	**AUTHOR'S NOTE**
7	**ALICE, SWEET ALICE (1976)**
9	**ANGEL HEART (1987)**
11	**Interview with actor Mickey Rourke**
12	**ANTHROPOPHAGUS (1981)**
14	**BLOODY MOON (1981)**
15	**BRITAIN'S BARON OF BLOOD: A CONVERSATION WITH NORMAN J. WARREN**
23	**A BUCKET OF BLOOD (1959)**
25	**Interview with producer/director Roger Corman**
27	**CHOSEN SURVIVORS (1974)**
29	**CITY OF THE LIVING DEAD (1980)**
30	**Interview with composer Fabio Frizzi**
33	**THE COMPANY OF WOLVES (1984)**
35	**Interview with actor Stephen Rea**
37	**COUNT DRACULA'S GREAT LOVE (1972)**
40	**DAUGHTERS OF DARKNESS (1971)**
41	**Interview with director Harry Kumel**
43	**Interview with actress Danielle Ouimet**
44	**DEMON SEED (1977)**
46	**THE DEVIL'S NIGHTMARE (1971)**
47	**Interview with composer Allesandro Allessandroni**
49	**IN THE FOLDS OF THE FLESH (1970)**

51	**THE KEEP (1983)**
53	**LAIR OF THE WHITE WORM (1988)**
55	**Interview with actress Amanda Donohoe**
57	**LAND OF THE MINOTAUR (1976)**
59	**THE LAST MAN ON EARTH (1964)**
61	**Interview with writer Richard Matheson**
62	**LEGEND OF THE WEREWOLF (1975)**
64	**LIFEFORCE (1985)**
65	**Interview with director Tobe Hooper**
68	**THE LIVING DEAD AT THE MANCHESTER MORGUE (1974)**
71	**THE MANY LIVES OF MARK DAMON**
75	**MAXIMUM OVERDRIVE (1986)**
77	**NOMADS (1986)**
79	**NOSFERATU: PHANTOM DER NACHT (1979)**
82	**PSYCHOMANIA (1971)**
83	**Interview with composer John Cameron**
84	**PSYCHO III (1986)**
87	**RAVENOUS (1999)**
90	**THE SENTINEL (1977)**
93	**Interview with director Michael Winner**
94	**THE SOUND OF SHOCK: A BRIEF HISTORY OF CANADIAN COMPOSER PAUL ZAZA**
98	**THE SHOUT (1975)**
101	**SOLE SURVIVOR (1983)**

AUTHOR'S NOTE

So.

You've bought my *Blood Spattered Book*.

Thank you. It means a lot.

Maybe some of you know me, know my writing, know my leanings.

If you do, then you're aware that the kinds of films I adore tend to play within the cinematic confines of what we call "horror." More importantly, the kinds of films I adore aren't perfect at all but rather are flawed features that nonetheless defy expectations and occasionally reach the sublime heights that only genuine works of accidental art can reach.

Essentially, I like movies that misbehave.

This *Blood Spattered Book* will spotlight a selection of my personal favorite filmed fever dreams; underrated horror, dark fantasy and cult genre pictures that aren't quite mainstream and in some cases are woefully obscure and/or unfairly maligned by many.

Most, if any, of these wonderful pictures have never made any serious critic's top-10-of-all-time-list but then again, I've never claimed to be a 'serious' critic. I know what I like, however, and each and every one of these mad movies means something to me personally. They have, in some way, shape or form, contributed to who I am as a writer, an artist and a lover of cinema at large. Many of them continue to shape the course of my life and I have no intention in stopping them from doing so.

Some of these essays have been re-tooled from existing entries in my *Blood Spattered Blog*, the weekly online column I write for *www.Fangoria.com*. Many are brand new. And just for kicks, I've thrown in some exclusive interviews with a few genuine cult film icons, some of whom have rarely been grilled about their work in horror but who kindly chimed in for the specific purpose of making this book as (hopefully) brilliant as it is.

If I've done my job right, by the end of this unapologetically enthusiastic tome, you'll have fallen in love with these films and the people who made them. Perhaps some of your own guilty celluloid pleasures will have been vindicated. Maybe you'll think I'm out to lunch. Either way, I hope you find this *Blood Spattered Book* to be an entertaining, amusing, heartfelt and visually interesting reference guide, one written by a lifelong, unapologetic horror film fan *for* lifelong, unapologetic horror film fans.

Bon appétit…

ALICE, SWEET ALICE
1976

Starring Linda Miller, Paula Sheppard and Brooke Shields
Written by Rosemary Ritvo and Alfred Sole
Directed by Alfred Sole

The fact that film history barely acknowledges co-writer/director Alfred Sole's sophisticated, unbelievably disturbing 1976 dark thriller/murder mystery *Alice, Sweet Alice* as a major work of psychological horror, is patently ridiculous and borderline offensive. The grim, grisly and offbeat movie (originally released under the title *Communion* then re-issued as *Holy Terror* before getting stuck with the moniker it now bears) is an eerie, emotionally draining and thoroughly fascinating picture that needs far more love ladled on it than the lowly level it now seems to command.

Sole's prickly, melodramatic fractured masterpiece tells the tale of New Jersey divorcee Catherine Spages (Linda Miller) and her two daughters, sweet little Karen (played by a pre-*Pretty Baby* Brooke Shields in her movie debut) and the slightly older (and more-than-slightly disturbed) Alice (Paula Sheppard, who would grow up to star in the counterculture punk rock/sci-fi classic *Liquid Sky*). Seems Alice is none too pleased by the fact that her cherub-faced sibling gets most of the attention from not only her mom, but also from her shrill, overbearing aunt, her grossly obese, potentially pedophilic landlord and even the far-too-attentive parish priest. She displays this displeasure physically, with an endless array of tantrums, meltdowns and sister-baiting torments that further marginalize her into the realms of the less loved. The fact that the doted-on Karen is all set to receive her very first communion, something that had always been denied to Alice because she was born out of wedlock, thus being deemed illegitimate by the Catholic church, is the final straw and almost pushes the jealous, ever-slighted girl over the proverbial edge.

Then, on the very day she is designated to ritualistically eat the body of Christ, little Karen is murdered (a brutal, shocking, yet effectively bloodless sequence in which Shields is choked with a candle, stuffed in a drawer and set on fire). Almost immediately, suspicion universally falls squarely upon the sloped shoulders of the gloomy, unstable Alice whose increasingly oddball behavior appears to implicate her beyond a shadow of a doubt.

But as more and more members of the Spages family and those that surround them fall prey to a diminutive, plastic-masked, butcher knife-wielding, yellow rain-slicker-wearing homicidal lunatic (who has a similar visual presence to the elusive red-coated killer-dwarf in Nicholas Roeg's masterful *Don't Look Now*), we quickly learn that the ties that bind are tenuous at best

Alice (Paula Sheppard) is unmasked by her mother (Linda Miller)

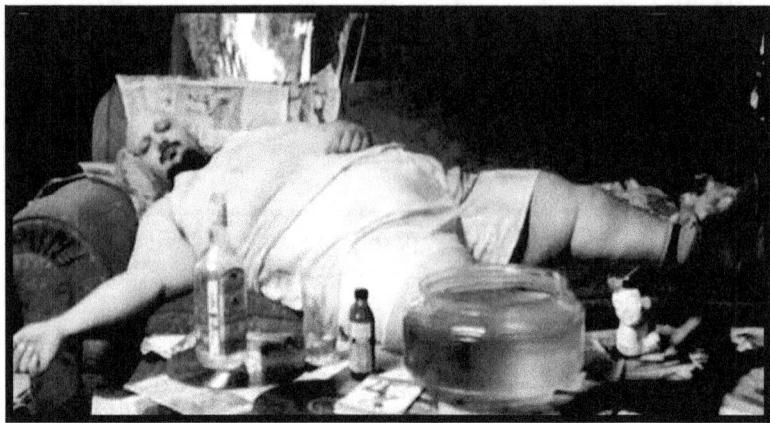
The repellent Mr. Alphonso (Alphonso DeNoble)

Brooke Shields as Karen in *Alice, Sweet Alice*

and that the church's guilt-ridden stranglehold on its flock runs deep…and runs red.

Alice, Sweet Alice is often dismissed as a "slasher" movie and is sometimes cited as being the closest American cousin to the Italian giallo film, but these are merely surface observations. The picture is much closer to Hitchcock than *Halloween* and where the vintage giallo thrillers of Mario Bava and Dario Argento favor a more style over substance aesthetic, *Alice, Sweet Alice* has both of these driving, defining cinematic elements in sanguinary spades. Director Sole (who incidentally is the uncle of indie horror filmmaker Dante Tomaseli) displays a sure hand at weaving obsessive imagery and boasts an almost Polanski-esque ability to milk queasy, sinister unease out of the working-class urban lifestyle, creating an ever present aura of onscreen, everyday dread and a sense that the world these people inhabit is irrevocably bent and forever off its axis.

The film has a unique narrative rhythm as well, with the central mystery resolving itself almost halfway through only to evolve from a "whodunit" to "why-dunit." Though this tonal shift is initially jarring, it's a testament to the picture's power (and Sole's ace direction) that it manages to keep you completely hooked—sometimes reluctantly so—right up until the final, chilling shot.

Credit must also go to composer Stephen Lawrence's rich, elegant and genuinely creepy Bernard Herrmann-esque neo-classical score that's subtly effective when it needs to be and terrifyingly aggressive during the frequent shock scenes. But what truly gives the remarkable *Alice, Sweet Alice* its frightening fingerprint is the amazing rogues gallery of offbeat characters that slither around the picture's claustrophobic corners. Sheppard was actually 19 when she was asked to play the role of the titular, possibly murderous preteen and this visibly wizened, physical maturity gives Alice an effectively world-weary, tragically grotesque presence, especially when she's nicking her baby sister's dollies or choking Mr. Alphonso's kittens.

Ah yes…Mr. Alphonso…

The pasty, obscenely overweight landlord and filthy, cat-cradling shut-in has to be seen to be believed. Played by the long-MIA character actor Alphonso DeNoble (Joel M. Reed's indefensible exploitation classic *Bloodsucking Freaks*), Mr. Alphonso is one of sick cinema's most stomach-churning pseudo-villains. Whether fanning his greasy, sweaty, repellent self in an easy chair while listening to opera, feeding his horde of mangy, mewling felines or lecherously pawing at Alice, his is a creation of brilliant slobbery and is just one of the many morally repellent adult characters that litter the film.

And perhaps it's that lack of a clearly defined protagonist that has kept *Alice, Sweet Alice* at an arm's distance to many a film lover: there's nobody to really root for in this movie, just a joyless bunch of terrified, religion-damaged, working-class hypocrites, who offer up their children to the altar of Christ without conscience…and suffer gravely for it.

***Alice, Sweet Alice*'s eerie, diminutive masked killer**

ANGEL HEART
1987

Starring Mickey Rourke, Robert DeNiro and Lisa Bonet
Based on the Novel by William Hjortsberg
Written and Directed by Alan Parker

While the study and obsession of the horror movie essentially defines a good chunk of my identity, let it be known that I am a great lover of ALL genre films, especially Westerns and perhaps even more so, that shadowy, morally ambiguous brand of pulp cinema that the French collectively called Film Noir.

You know what I mean.

The kind of early, expressionist-influenced, American crime and detective cinema that intentionally blurred the previously pretty clear lines between hero and villain. The best noir paints grim, sexually caustic portraits of a corrupt and rotten world, giving us duplicitous women and greasy protagonists that are just as conflicted and depraved as the double dealing scumbags that they have sworn to bring down.

But I'm not a purist by any stretch and it's always a treat for me to see a more modern approach that opts to play with the form, cannily copping from a myriad of eras, styles and genres, mashing them together with grace, style, wit, and occasionally, bold, brilliant and ballsy moviemaking bravado. And Alan (*Pink Floyd's The Wall, Midnight Express*) Parker's one-of-a-kind masterpiece of neo-noir, the jet black 1987 mood piece *Angel Heart*, does this better than any other film I've seen.

New York, 1955. A grimy, suffocating post-war metropolis whose labyrinthine streets and dirty back alleys skid row gumshoe Harry Angel (the effortlessly engaging Mickey Rourke) reluctantly calls home. Angel's life is a nickel and dime world of cheap crooks, cheating husbands and insurance scams; a patchwork of pickup snoop jobs that barely sustain his livelihood... that is until he meets the mysterious Louis Cyphre (Robert DeNiro). A suave, decadent, sophisticated, moneyed and dangerous presence, the finely tailored (and sharply manicured) Cyphre commissions the down-but-not-quite-out Angel to locate a once-famous, now-forgotten crooner named Johnny Favorite. Seems this ever-so-slightly sinister gentleman gave the MIA Favorite some kind of career boost before the war and now he wants to collect on the debt.

Without a flicker of hesitation, Angel accepts the high-paying job and, as the ensuing Harlem and New Orleans-bound trails toward Favorite run both hot and cold (and often, very wet and red), he soon finds himself knee deep in a melting pot of bloody murder, taboo sex, Satanism, voodoo rites and human sacrifice. As he sinks deeper and deeper into an emotional (and increasingly likely *supernatural*) quagmire, Angel begins to seriously question his sanity...and ultimately, his very identity.

Based on the amount of times I have revisited this film since I first saw it on unrated home video back in 1988, I'd have to go on record and say that *Angel Heart* (itself

9

Angel Heart **publicity still featuring Lisa Bonet striking a sultry, sweaty pose**

based on William Hjortsberg's equally deft, but tonally different novel *Falling Angel*) is my all-time favorite movie, full stop.

There are many reasons why this is so. Allow me to testify…

First of all, Rourke is phenomenal. It's perhaps somewhat difficult for some of you to recall, but there was a time in the '80s when Mickey Rourke was MICKEY FUCKING ROURKE; the baddest-ass outlaw actor since Marlon Brando. Edgy roles in decade-defining flicks like *Diner, The Pope of Greenwich Village, Barfly* and *Year of the Dragon* garnered him a reputation as both rough and intense, yet sympathetic screen presence; an actor who demanded and commanded high critical accolades and deserved amounts of audience attention.

But bad project choices (*Wild Orchid, Harley Davidson and the Marlboro Man* and virtually every film he did in the 1990s) and worse career deviances (the oddest boxer since Uwe Boll…or me!) derailed his professional life, until his *Marv*-elous brute thug turn in Robert Rodriguez's instant cult classic *Sin City* and his remarkable, multi award-winning turn in Darren Aronofsky's searing character study *The Wrestler* stuck him back on the map. But in *Angel Heart* he's at his stubbly faced, reckless best, creating a character that is alternately sleazy, sweet, tragic, funny and unintentionally cruel; a relentlessly inventive, brooding and self-destructive tragic anti-hero right out of Dashiell Hammett or Mickey Spillane.

The supporting performances in *Angel Heart* are aces across the board too, with ex-*Cosby Show* kid Lisa Bonet the picture of coquettish sexuality (and whose graphic, chicken blood-soaked sex scene with Rourke landed the picture in hot water with the MPAA and pooched her professional relationship with the notoriously controlling Bill Cosby). DeNiro, all sharp nails and evil *Taxi Driver*–era Martin Scorsese beard, simply oozes eerie elegance and palpable menace. And real deal blues man Brownie McGhee adds authentic Creole edge as the doomed guitar man and voodoo disciple Toots Sweet while British actress Charlotte Rampling's walk leaves a sultry, dangerous impact.

Then there's Trevor Jones' absolutely chilling, experimental score; a meltdown of deep drones, disconnected whispers, Courtney Pine's dissonant saxophone stings and fragmented haunting 1930s crooner tunes (specifically Glen Gray's big band chestnut "Girl of My Dreams") that continually washes over Parker's hypnotic, obsessive images from the minute the film fades into its shocking, opening gutter/murder scene to Angel's credit-crawl elevator descent, gelling them together with an unsettling level of inevitable dread that is nothing short of sweet suffocation. (Incidentally, the out-of-print soundtrack album released on the Island Records imprint is laid out like a single-track concept album and is just as vital as the picture it supports.)

Angel Heart isn't just a deeply scary, psychosexual slice of slick, gruesome gothic noir—though it is most assuredly that too. At its core it's a kind of cinematic whirlpool; a sucking, swirling, pulsing, painfully protracted peek into the heart of supreme inner darkness that bonds us all, sucking the viewer down, down, down into its murky vortex. It's a finely orchestrated nightmare in which the audience's perceptions of where the truth truly lies become as profoundly skewed as the final fate of poor old Harry Angel…er, Johnny Favorite, um…Harry. Johnny. Harry...

Robert DeNiro as Louis Cyphre oozes evil in *Angel Heart*.

AN INTERVIEW WITH ACTOR MICKEY ROURKE

Note: The following conversation took place in November 2008, two months before Rourke won the best actor Golden Globe and BAFTA Awards for *The Wrestler*.

After essentially monopolizing the market in edgy movies like Angel Heart *in the 1980s you had—by your own admission—some dark days, both personally and professionally...*

Fuck, yeah.

Did you ever think that you'd make a comeback?

No. I mean, I was on the bench for 13 years and after 10 years goes by you start to think, man, is it really fucking over like everyone says it is? I'd be at a convenience store in LA at 2 in the morning and some guy would say, "Weren't you in *Angel Heart* or *9 1/2 Weeks?*" and I'd be like, Christ, just let me get my fucking cigarettes and get the fuck outta here! They'd say, "What happened to you?" "Why don't you work anymore?" I had to hear that shit 24/7...

Well, there were lots of us out there—myself included—who followed your career everywhere, regardless where it went. Stuff like Double Team, Bullet...

Right, the shit, yeah.

Not all of it was shit. Bullet *had some great moments. But didn't that fan support, all those websites and blogs, help prop you up? Give you hope?*

You mean now?

No, then...

No...no...because that's what you *did*. You can't pay your rent on that. You can't get laid on that. I was yesterday's news.

Everyone's citing Darren Aronofsky's The Wrestler *as your resurrection. But after the boxing misstep, the well-publicized breakup of your marriage to Carré Otis, it was a long process to get your career back on track...*

Yeah, it was. I mean there were small things along the way that helped. Sean Penn went out of his way to give me a day's work on *The Pledge*. Sly Stallone saw me eating at a restaurant where I could barely pay for my spaghetti and he put me in *Get Carter*. Tony Scott gave me *Domino* and *Man On Fire*. Robert Rodriguez gave me some time on that Mexican movie (*Once Upon a Time in Mexico*) and *Sin City*. I was lucky to have that help.

Were things really that bad for you financially?

Well, I remember back in L.A., I sold all my motorcycles to pay my rent and I called up a friend to get a construction job, thinking if I could work in the valley, no one would recognize me. He said, "Mickey, I'm really busy, I don't have time for your shit right now!" And I thought, Jesus Christ, I can't even get a construction job! I was pretty low.

But now you're back, winning awards and wooing critics and your fans feel vindicated. How do you *feel?*

When you've been out of work for a decade or so, you're wary of it all. I mean, I behaved so badly when I had my first chance— I wasn't accountable, I wasn't responsible, I wasn't professional. It wasn't that I was misunderstood, I just behaved terribly. I had this fuse burning inside of me and I didn't have the knowledge how to fix that and only when you have that knowledge—which I do now—can you make a change.

*And the offers post-*The Wrestler, *are they getting better?*

Well, Hollywood's not exactly running at my door yet...but we'll see.

Hard-boiled Harry Angel (Mickey Rourke) cocks his pistol.

ANTHROPOPHAGUS 1981

Starring Tisa Farrow, George Eastman and
Serena Grandi
Written by Joe D'Amato and George Eastman
Directed by Joe D'Amato

Uncle Chas, this one's for you...

Even if you're only a casual fan of vintage, "video nasty"-era Italian terror, chances are you've at the very least heard of exploitation director Joe D'Amato's sickening and sloppy paean to Mediterranean cannibal madness, the dire, dreaded and somewhat undervalued *Anthropophagus*.

Although this notorious slab of sleaze has been corrupting both the innocent and not-so-innocent under a myriad of titles since its release in 1981, my introduction to its considerable charms came via a wallow in the stained pages of *Gorezone*. For those few lucky lads and ladies who may recall, *Gorezone* was the failed sister magazine to *Fangoria* (the periodical I currently scribble for) and in it was a column by a journalist who pretty much paved the path for virtually everything I've done with a pen in my professional life. The man's name was Chas. Balun and the incredible column he wrote was called "Piece o' Mind."

Every month, without fail, Balun—a devout hippie and gory horror enthusiast—would write the most disarmingly *alive* gonzo words about whatever splatter flick (usually hailing from Europe) that was lighting his fire at that particular time. In one typically entertaining entry, he opted to prattle about a low-end sleaze auteur named Joe D'Amato; specifically a naughty little number he made called *The Grim Reaper*. Now, Balun had the very special gift of making even the lowliest of genre offerings seem like so much bloody gold and his words about *The Grim Reaper* both sold me and scared me. Apparently this was one picture that bit back.

So I searched and I searched and eventually, I managed to secure a deplorable looking UK bootleg print of the picture titled *Anthropophagus: The Beast*. Slightly cut and borderline watchable, the battered and mangled version I saw still managed to mess me up proper and it stuck to my ribs like coagulated oatmeal.

Recently, an Italian pal of mine sent me a pristine and uncut copy of the film and I'm happy to report that *Anthropophagus* is as cheerfully putrid now as it was then.

The film stars Tisa Farrow (sister of Mia and starlet of Lucio Fulci's immortal 1979 film *Zombie*) as a wide-eyed American tourist who, while on vacation with her pals in prettier than humanly possible Greece, decides on a whim to visit a nearby island that's been cut off from the rest of the country. Seems the said isle is completely deserted, save for a shell-shocked lass in a nearby abandoned mansion, who keeps babbling on about a beast that's prowling about the place looking for victims. She's right, of course. A beefy, putty-faced man-eating monstrosity, played by George Eastman (from many a D'Amato joint, including the legendary porn-horror *Erotic Nights of the Living Dead* and who also co-produced this creeper) as a Frankenstein-like lunatic, has apparently killed and eaten every living thing on the island and is now tracking our intrepid, invasive heroes with lethal intent to snack.

If you've ever seen a non-porn D'Amato picture (his real, non-anglicized name, incidentally, is Aristide Masseccesi) then you probably have an idea what to expect from *Anthropophagus*: cheap production values, leering cinematography, brutish, cruel, humorless narrative sensibilities and buckets of outrageous, sloppy violence. Outside of his ultra-disturbing necro-romance *Buio Omega* (arguably his finest work), *Anthropophagus* is perhaps D'Amato's queasiest, slimiest and, ultimately, scariest film. This is a relentlessly dark, mean and nihilistic picture, one whose outlook on the world is far from pleasant and whose sole purpose it seems, is to make you sick. And it works.

The chief reason this movie ran into so much international censorial difficulties are two unbelievably, almost supernaturally sickening sequences that turned tummies and caused more conservative countries to shave them down and, in some cases (as in England, during the infamous government-sanctioned "video nasty" craze), cut them from the prints entirely. In one of them, Eastman's brutish titular menace (*Anthrophagus* means, literally, cannibal) corners one of the put-upon tourists, who just happens to be with child, and,

The Anthrophagus (George Eastman) has atrocious table manners.

in a Tate/Manson murders twist, rips the squirming fetus from her living womb as she shrieks away in horror.

Eastman then proceeds to scarf down the unborn child, umbilical cord and all. It's a cheap, nauseating effect that pushes the boundaries of, um, good taste and is guaranteed to send expectant mothers howling for the exits in outrage.

The other less offensive, but far stranger, stretch occurs at the climax, where the now dying, almost defeated monster collapses, and with nary a victim in site, rips out his own guts and valiantly tries to eat himself! It's an insane set piece to be sure, but it also serves to illustrate how dedicated D'Amato is in his quest to shock.

Outside of these incredible sequences, *Anthropophagus* is padded out with all manner of madness that fans of these films devour like so many of Eastman's human hors d'oeuvres. There's loads of excess blood and gore, including a scalp-ripping effect whose shoddiness only adds to the yuck factor; there's the gleefully inept, zombified performances by the terminally confused international cast; there's a fantastic, completely inappropriate electronic music score by D'Amato regular Marcello Giombini; there's exquisite location footage and eerie illustrations of the natural world inhabited by something horrifically unnatural.

Is *Anthropophagus* a good movie? Depends on your definition. I think D'Amato (who passed away in 1999) was too unsophisticated a filmmaker to concern himself with something as bourgeoisie as, y'know, quality cinema. He approached horror the same way he approached pornography: simply pointing the camera and honing in on various squirting fluids, penetrations and gynecology. But he also had an almost animalistic instinct to show the unshowable with a bleak, primal power. *Anthropophagus* is slow, severe, sickening and truly upsetting. It stays with you long after the last of Eastman's spleen falls from his blood-crusted lips.

The above European lobby cards display an alternate release title for *Anthropophagus*.

BLOODY MOON 1981

Starring Olivia Pascal, Alexander Waechter and
Christopher Moosbrugger
Written by Rayo Casablanca
Directed by Jesus Franco

The weird and wonderful work of controversial genre filmmaking legend Jesus "Jess" Franco came to my attention via an article in *Fangoria*. It was in the late '80s when I was in my early teens that one of my favorite *Fango* scribes, Tim Lucas, had scribbled a piece based on his intrepid investigations into the serpentine oeuvre of the elusive Eurotrash auteur. It was a fascinating column, one that attempted to differentiate between authentic Francos, those he merely had a hand in creatively, and the myriad of none-too-clever forgeries.

Reading Lucas' words was akin to following a sort of cinema-obsessed Indiana Jones down a spiraling wormhole of weird movie bliss. It was my first master class in the mind boggling world of vintage international exploitation filmmaking and perhaps more profoundly, it made me aware of how crass exhibitors worldwide would tailor those pictures to suit or sneak around the social taboos of their home countries.

Born in Spain in 1930, Jess Franco first made his major mark in France with a series of crisp, sleazy black and white art house horror pictures like 1962's *The Awful Dr. Orloff* (a vague rip-off of Georges Franju's groundbreaking sex and surgery epic *Eyes Without A Face*), movies that valued high contrast photography, graphic violence and abundant female nudity. Over the span of the ensuing decade the tirelessly prolific Franco would make scores of personal, jazz influenced (Franco was also an accomplished composer and musician) sonnets to sex and gore, playing with color and working with budgets both high and low in any country that would fund his filmmaking fetish.

Which brings me to *Bloody Moon*, a later-period early-'80s German-financed (the original title was *Die Sage Des Todes*) bloodbath made in the wake of the slasher craze sparked by John Carpenter's *Halloween* and juiced up by the considerably later, much more explicit *Friday the 13th*. But the seriously bent *Bloody Moon* is so much more than simply a stalk-and-stab shocker. Why? Because it was made by Franco, of course and, as any serious scholar of Jess' work knows, no matter how loathsome and cheap a Franco film can be (unwatchable crap like *Revenge In the House of Usher* immediately and painfully springs to mind), there's always *something* there that's uniquely his. A lazy lidded energy, a leering point of view…something.

The typically greasy-looking film opens on a spectacularly sickening murder at a Spanish girls school by a completely un-spectacularly made up lunatic (the "special effects" applied to his puss amount to so much melted cheese). Five years later, pretty young student Angela (softcore starlet Olivia Pascal) has taken up residence in the same room where the said slaughter went down and to make matters eerier, the Velveeta-faced killer has been released from the looney bin, apparently none to reformed.

Sooner than later, a spate of increasingly sadistic killings kicks into high gear with all manner of lovely lasses getting revoltingly ripped to ribbons. Is it old gouda-face wearing the Argento-esque black gloves that pop into frame before each offing? Is it his comely sister with whom he shares a rather, um, close relationship? Before Franco's 90-minute mess winds down, all questions will be answered and many tummies will be well turned…

Above: Sylvia Pascal is about to get the point of starring in a Franco film...
Below: *Bloody Moon*'s black-gloved killer likes to keep his victims fresh.

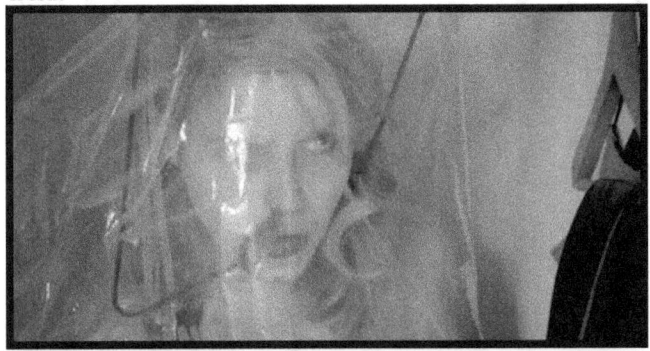

Foreplay to the money shot that caused *Bloody Moon* so much trouble with the UK censors.

Now, as I mentioned, Franco made a staggering amount of films, including such acknowledged classics like *Venus in Furs, She Killed in Ecstasy, Faceless* and *Vampyros Lesbos*, so you might be wondering why I've chosen to muse on *Bloody Moon*. The answer is simple. Plenty of people despise the work of Jess Franco, laughingly labeling him a hack. And while I'll never argue that the man has made more than his share of duds, when someone gives him a bit of time—and more importantly, money—Franco can make stylish eccentric and commercially competent genre junk food with style and verve. And this grisly, goofy little shocker is nothing if not loads of lively, livid fun.

By his own admission (revealed in an interview that accompanies a recent DVD re-issue release from the Severin label), Franco signed on to the project under the promise that his craven producers had art rock super group Pink Floyd attached to compose the score. As this was the early '80s and the already legendary band was achieving their commercial apex with the double disc, chart-topping album *The Wall*, it would be obvious to anyone with any shade of cynicism or insight that they would never, *ever* have their name glued to a grubby European slasher movie directed by the guy who made *The Bare Breasted Countess*.

So instead of a Floyd score, *Bloody Moon* features music by someone named Gerhard Heinz, a German-born tunesmith who tries his best to mimic a David Gilmour-esque psych-rock sound and for the most part, succeeds. Many fans and critics have cited this score as the picture's most atrocious flaw, but I rather like it—it's bizarre, bombastic and dirty...and it works. When an unlucky lady gets her head sawed off in the film's most notorious (and delightfully fake) gore sequence, those wailing guitars and skunky bass lines sound perfectly awesome.

A masterpiece? Far from it. But *Bloody Moon* is pure, sleazy, upbeat Franco. A document of a creative innocent, a guy who worked to live and lived to work, who just loved making movies and managed to weave his way into pop culture legend by never giving up, never stepping off that ladder. Good on him...

BRITAIN'S BARON OF BLOOD: A CONVERSATION WITH NORMAN J. WARREN

June 2008

The eccentric exploitation films of British filmmaker Norman J. Warren first fell onto my radar by way of a nasty little used number I bought for next to nothing at a greasy mom and pop video store in West Toronto. The film in question was called *Horror Planet*, a 90-minute Warren-directed, *Alien*-inspired ode to intergalactic sex and violence featuring a horny reptilian space beastie who humps humans in a desperate attempt to make more of his kind.

Eventually, after a bit of research, I learned that *Horror Planet* was in fact the U.S. handle slapped on the picture by the theatrical distributor (in this case, Avco-Embassy) and the movie's true title was the considerably more lurid (and appropriate) *Inseminoid*.

I began tracking down other Warren wonders, stuff like the erotic nickel-and-dime human-hungry spaceman

A very young Norman J. Warren calls the saucy shots.

shocker *Alien Prey* (or just *Prey* if you live in the UK), the silly but endearing late period *Bloody New Year* and most impressively, the absolutely crazed movie-within-a-movie supernatural gore-fest *Terror*. I found out that Warren's roots were in short films and eventually included, as many European genre director's early credits did, softcore porn comedies and that a childhood battle with polio rendered him with the use of only one arm.

But I knew very little about the man himself, about what made him tick and why he'd committed all those charming silver screen sins that have stuck around to please miscreants such as myself.

A lengthy conversation cleared up many of those mysteries. Here, dear readers, is that very conversation…

After your initial short film experiments in the mid '60s, your first feature-length picture was 1968's Her Private Hell…*a naughty film, no?*

Yes, it was! There were of course many films like it around from Germany and Sweden, "sexploitation films" we called them then and still do, but none really that were made in England. So when *Her Private Hell* came along, it suddenly became this enormous hit and I think that it was because it was homegrown. It was also one of the first sex films to really tell a coherent story. So while it was still pretty far from being a great film, it was unique and box office-wise, it was an amazing hit, which did me a world of good, I assure you!

The BBFC have always been notorious for their hatred of horror…but what were their views on the sexploitation film? How much could you show without getting your figurative knuckles rapped?

If you were to see *Her Private Hell* now, it would seem innocent, naïve and really, it was never that bad. But still,

Video art for Warren's weird-and-sleazy sci-fi sex-romp *Prey*.

just loved movies in general. My mother used to take me to the movies and we would watch everything, all kinds of films, all genres, including all the old Lugosi and Karloff pictures, which were then considered quite gentle. When it came to more extreme horror though, I think you had to be either 16 or 17 to get into horror pictures theatrically so I had to wait awhile. The first horror stuff that really hit me was Hammer—*Curse of Frankenstein* in 1957 and then *Dracula* the following year, both of which hit everybody in the UK in a BIG way.

So when it came time to make Slave *were you intentionally referencing those sorts of pictures that Hammer specialized in?*

We were actually trying to move away from that Hammer style, which by that time was becoming rather passé, but at the same time there was some reference to them; the upper- middle-class families who live in these big houses but seemingly have no jobs. Just some of the character styling. In our film however we went considerably farther with the sex.

the censor was very particular about what you could put onscreen. If you had a bare breast you couldn't show the nipple. And of course the guy still had to keep his pants on in bed or else you had to cover him with a sheet. So it was a very innocent time. My film did run into trouble, however, even though most of my nudity was only shown from the rear. I made only one more sexploitation film called *Loving Feeling* the following year—in color and in Cinemascope—and by that time the censor had relaxed. We could at this point show the nipple and show SOME female frontal nudity. Things were beginning to change…

Your first horror film was 1976's Satan's Slave *with one of my favorite British character actors, Michael Gough. Had you been a fan of the genre before this point?*

Well yes, but not any more than other movies really. I mean, all little boys are attracted to horror to some extent…probably because horror movies are the first ones to be forbidden by your parents. But I must confess that I

Lobby card for the demented, *Suspiria*-inspired shocker *Terror*

Looking back on Satan's Slave *today, what do you think about it?*

I'm still happy to watch it and I think it works very well for what we trying to do and considering the limitations we had to deal with. *Satan's Slave* was one of two times I teamed up with (producer and cinematographer) Les Young. We'd been trying to get financing from various people for over a year and a half to no avail so finally we just took the gamble and did it ourselves. Fortunately for us, it paid off.

My favorite of your films is without a doubt 1978's Terror. *It's utterly mad. I've read that you were a fan of Dario Argento's immortal* Suspiria *at the time.*

Very much so, yes. I went to see *Suspiria* not knowing exactly what I was going to experience and I was promptly blown away. Basically Argento went against all the genre conventions of the time with that film; it was completely unique. I mean, when you analyze it, it doesn't make any real sense but that's really beside the point. *Suspiria* is about the colors, the camera work and of course that incredible Goblin music. It was all atmosphere and tension. So when it came time to do *Terror*, I was very conscious of that, of being freed from logic and just do whatever you liked and it proved to be the right approach because *Terror* was incredibly successful, especially with the teenage market.

You've never been a darling of the critics. Were the British press ever cruel to you because of the pictures you were making?

Well, not cruel really, but to be honest it's always been the same climate in England. You see, horror has always been looked down upon and not deemed to be worth anyone's attention. So really, the critics just ignored me. There's a lot of snobbery in the UK about movies and especially the kind of movies I was making…

I love Inseminoid. *It's so gory and weird. I saw it first on home video as* Horror Planet…

A terrible title. I'm not sure why they put that title on the film at all.

I know. Inseminoid *just sounds so damn nasty. Speaking of, that film was released near the early days of the "Video Nasty" witch-hunt in the UK. Did you ever have any problems with the picture getting banned?*

We never did actually and *Inseminoid*, thankfully, never ended up on any "Video Nasty" list, but it WAS banned in Germany and it did get into some trouble in the press, but in ways that just helped the box office, really.

How so?

It got into hot water with various women's groups, especially with the graphic birth scenes. I think we re-

American poster art for the retitled *Inseminoid*

ally tapped into a very primal fear that pregnant women have—that they'll give birth to a monster—so we had women writing to the theatres trying to get the film banned! Again, it really helped sell tickets!

Inseminoid was obviously an attempt to ride the coattails of the success of Ridley Scott's Alien*...or am I wrong?*

You're wrong. We've always had this thing where people said we were copying *Alien* but that's simply just not true. The similarities between the two films were purely coincidental. I first got wind of the connection when 20th Century Fox started asking about *Inseminoid*; they wanted to screen it to see if it was a copy. It isn't at all and I was actually quite surprised when I finally got around to watching *Alien* that there were a few scenes that were similar. But we did not set out to copy Scott's film at all.

Inseminoid had such a wonderful cast...what are your recollections of Stephanie Beacham and Judy Geeson?

Not only is Stephanie Beacham an excellent actress and a very attractive woman, but she is also great fun to work with. Stephanie has a wonderful sense of humor and she can always see the funny side of any situation. She insisted on calling the film "Insecticide." With tongue firmly in cheek, she would often wind me up by asking what her motivation was for a particular action, just as I was about to call, "Action!" knowing full well that my answer would be, "Because it's in the script." But don't get me wrong, Stephanie was very professional and I could always count on her to give a good performance. We did get on very well, and we did have a lot of laughs during those long damp days in the caves.

The big delight for me was Judy Geeson.

She was an absolute joy to work with and just to be with. She had to play a very complex and demanding role, which in the hands of a less competent actress could easily have become comical. She also had to work in some awful conditions, but no matter how unpleasant the situ-

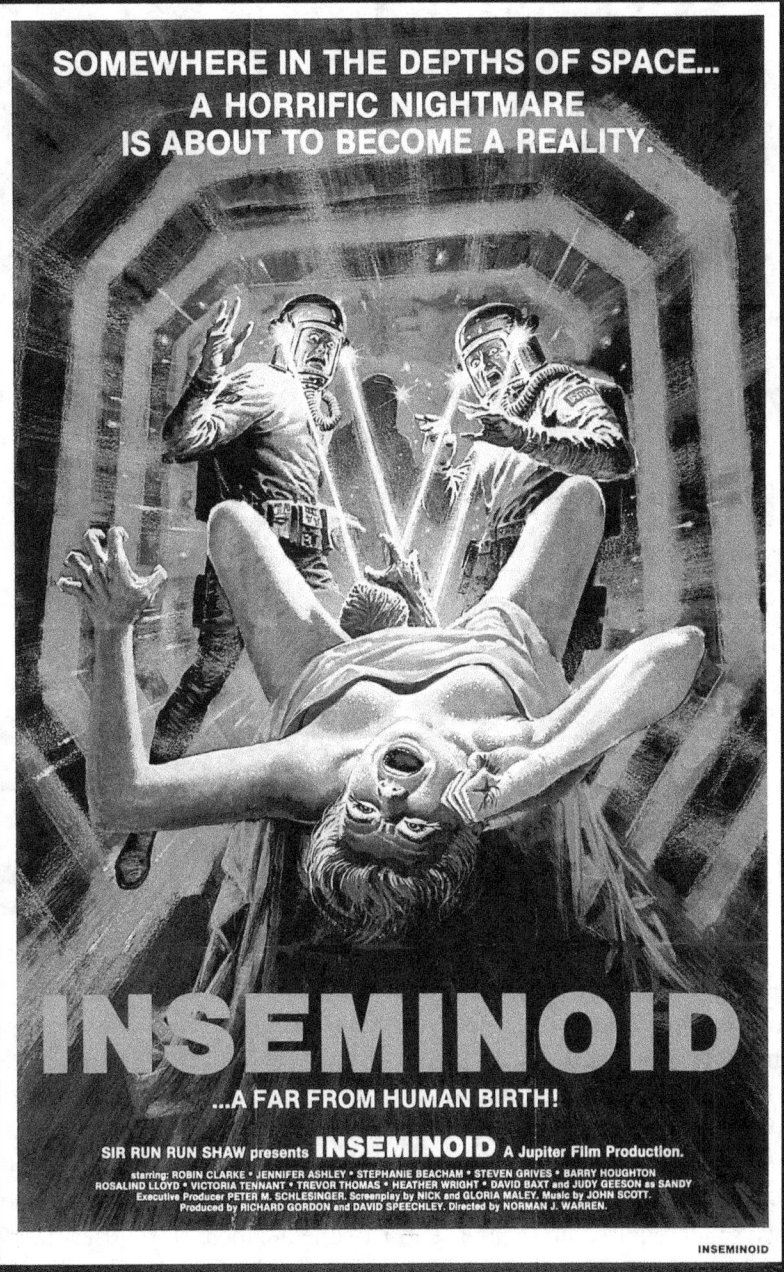

ation, she always gave me 100% effort and never-ending enthusiasm. She was prepared to work really hard every day and never had a word of complaint. The schedule only allowed her two days off, but rather than stay at home, she would still come to the location and help in any way she could. I really enjoyed working with Judy. She's a great actress and a very lovely person.

Who handled the FX for Inseminoid*?*

As with most films, there were several people involved in creating effects for *Inseminoid*. There were guys for explosions and gunshots, but to my shame I can't remember their names. Production designer Hayden Pearce created

Inseminoid's bastard beastie goes for the throat.

practical props like the touch burner, the small chainsaw and the small train. The wonderful baby monsters and the large monster, known to the cast and crew as "Big Daddy," were designed and created by Nick Maley, who also wrote the original script for *Inseminoid* with his actress wife, Gloria Walker. The baby monsters were amazing creations, which could move in a great many ways and required up to nine people to operate them. In the birth scene, the baby was able to grip Sandy's leg and pull itself out. Unfortunately, the British censor was not keen on this scene and would only allow it if the shots were cut. Sadly, the removed footage has been lost so I was unable to restore it for the box-set release. I would have liked to feature the baby monsters more in the film, but because they were very complex to operate and could take considerable time to set up, I could never allow enough time. The shooting schedule of just three weeks in the caves and one week in a studio was just too short to allow such luxuries.

Let's talk about the sci-fi/horror film you did prior to In-seminoid...*the sexy and eccentric exploitation gem* Prey, *or* Alien Prey, *as it's known in North America...*

Well that film has an interesting story. Terry Marcel, the producer, wanted to make a movie where an alien comes to earth, encounters lesbians and finds out humans are high in protein and easy prey and I agreed to direct it. But then they told me there was no script and we had to start filming in three weeks time! It was incredibly low budget and we had to shoot in only 10 days. There was just a hurriedly put together script. But it was quite an amazing experience and a lot of fun.

I've always thought of the film as a twisted, dirty cross between Nick Roeg's The Man Who Fell to Earth *and* Three's Company...

What's *Three's Company*?

Er...the American rip off of Man About the House...

Oh! Yes! It is actually! Well, certainly the Roeg connection was intentional. You know, I watched that film again and really liked it. It's been criticized for its slow pace, but I rather like that slow pace. And you know, we had the most perfect weather and those lovely, languid scenes of the two girls just wandering in the garden, enjoying the sun were proof of that. As ridiculous as the whole thing is, somehow it all seems to work, especially when the ending gets so violent.

How often do you re-visit your films?

Very rarely, actually. I only started to re-watch them in the early '90s, when several horror conventions began asking me to attend. Suddenly I was being approached by legions of fans of my work who wanted to know specific details about *Satan's Slave, Prey, Terror*...tons of fans that I didn't know existed! That's why I had to start looking at them again, just to prepare for these questions. Luckily, I still have all my old diaries, so now if anyone has a more in-depth question I can look it up.

Awesome!

No really, some of these young fans ask me all manner of strange questions! So it's nice to know I can properly answer them...

How does it feel being a cult hero?

It's very nice but it came as a total surprise. It's wonderful to know that the little pictures I did actually influenced people.

When people call you an exploitation filmmaker, how do you feel about that? How would you define an exploitation picture?

I have absolutely no problem with being referred to as an exploitation filmmaker, although I believe it's the wrong term. All films are exploitation films. We're all exploited pretty much all the time, by just about every industry. When I make a film, my main two aims are to entertain and make a return for the financer. So I guess a more suitable term would be, a 'commercial' director. Surely an exploitation picture is one that gives more of what you like.

What are your thoughts on the work of the "other" so-called British Horror New Wave director, Pete Walker?

I must confess I've not seen all of Pete Walker's film, but those that I have, I've really enjoyed. Pete's films are quite different to mine. He liked social subjects and would often make reference to the Catholic Church. I always felt he wanted to upset people, and it may seem

a strange thing to say, but in some ways his films have a documentary feel about them. Pete Walker certainly had his own style, and my two favorite films are *Frightmare* and *House of Whipcord*. Both were written by my old buddy David McGillivray.

Which one of your pictures stands as the one that you're most proud of?

That's a difficult question, because for various reasons I'm proud of most of my films. However, if I have to make a choice, it would be between *Terror* and *Inseminoid*. Both films were commercially successful, but for sheer enjoyment I would have to say *Terror* is my number one. Making a film can be extremely hard work, but at the same time it can also be fun, and I can honestly say that *Terror* was the most enjoyable and certainly the happiest film I have ever worked on. The same was felt by the entire cast and crew; it was just like a group of friends coming together to make a film and nobody really wanting it to end. We managed to achieve an enormous amount in just four weeks of shooting. Not just with scenes, which included action and effects, but also with the number of different sets and locations that were used. We seemed to be constantly on the move and loading and unloading equipment, just like a traveling circus.

What advice do you give to the aspiring horror filmmakers that approach you?

I simply tell them to never give up, to never stop trying to make movies and to get up and just get out there! Make movies! Follow your dreams!

Okay, Norman...the burning question that I'm sure everyone always asks you...

Go ahead…

Why haven't you made another movie since Bloody New Year? *Christ man! That was released in 1987!*

[Sigh] *Bloody New Year* was a very terrible experience for me; in fact it turned out to be a bloody nightmare. We had the wrong producers on that film and they didn't know anything about horror. So the film lacks in every department and by the end of it, my heart just wasn't in it. And my God, the soundtrack is appalling and there were no sound effects at all in it. They wanted to make the film cheaply and terribly quick. So at the end of that picture, I was disheartened for a while and walked away from things. I've tried several times to make another film, even in Hollywood, but they all just kept collapsing. Things changed. Everything has become corporations and committees…terrifying stuff and very much beyond me. But I'm still trying to get some stuff off the ground…

What would you do? Horror?

Yes, absolutely, but independent horror. I almost did a film in 2005, I was this close, but one person pulled out and the whole thing collapsed. Disheartening to say the least…

Would your film contain the kind of explicit violence today's audiences have come to expect in their horror films?

When it comes to graphic violence, I think we've had as much as we can take. Can it go farther? I mean, really, where will it end? I think we live in very violent times. But we can't blame horror, we can't blame TV, we can't blame games…it's a deeper issue. But done properly, violence in horror movies can be a wonderful tool…

What's your favorite movie of all time, Norman?

Beyond a shadow of a doubt, it has to be *Singin' in the Rain*…whenever I watch it, I'm happy again.

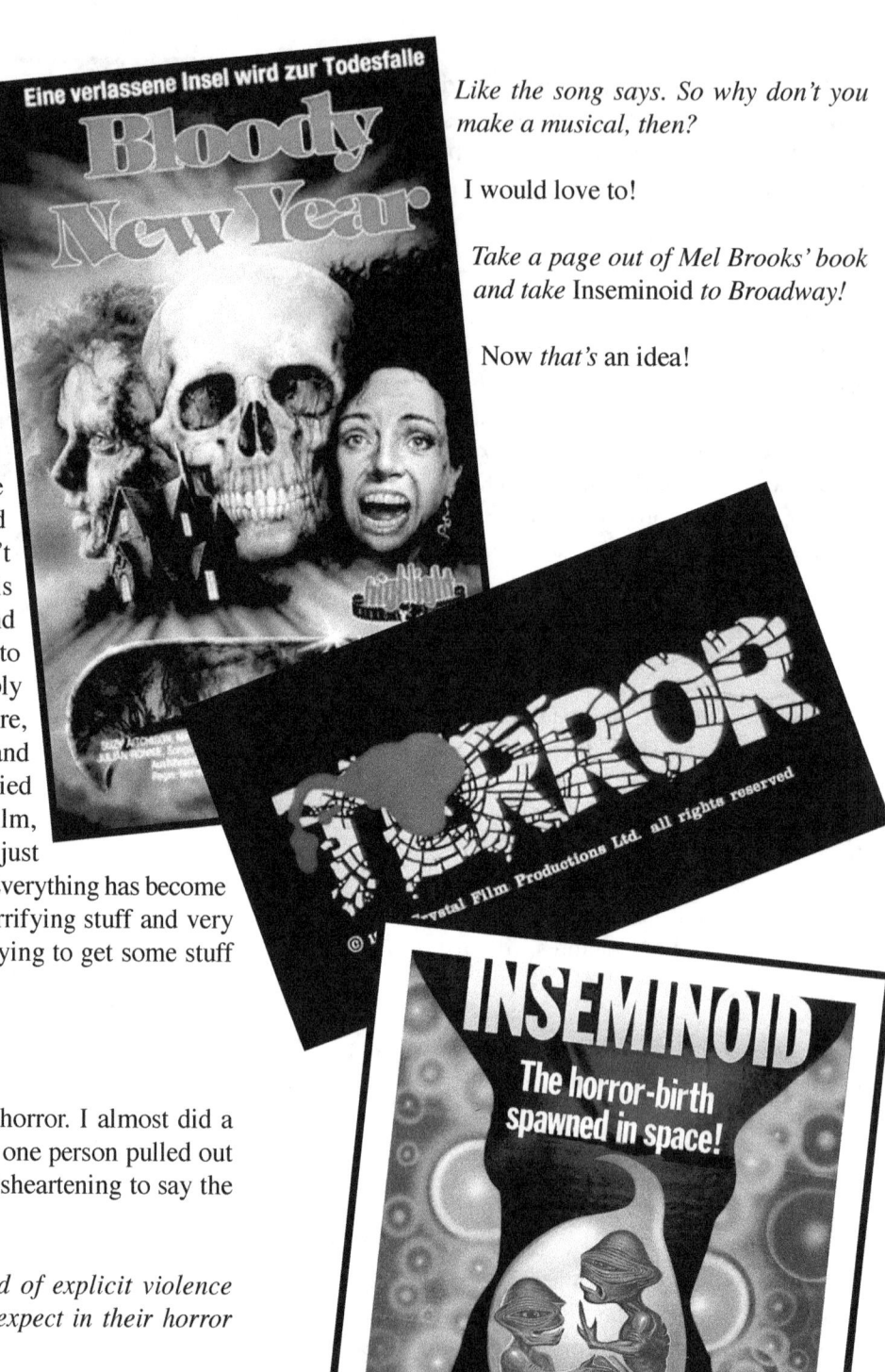

Like the song says. So why don't you make a musical, then?

I would love to!

Take a page out of Mel Brooks' book and take Inseminoid *to Broadway!*

Now *that's* an idea!

A BUCKET OF BLOOD 1959

Starring Dick Miller, Antony Carbone, Julian Burton
Written by Charles B. Griffith
Produced and Directed by Roger Corman

God bless Roger Corman.

That soft-spoken, seemingly ageless engineering student turned nickel-and-dime movie mogul has thrilled my cinematic sensibilities since I was able to read his name at the tail end of the opening credit-crawl on many a late night creature feature. Starting in the mid 1950s, Corman managed to sculpt a counter-culture cottage industry out of drive-in B-movie potboilers for the teenage market—films whose warm, cost-saving embraces would eventually nurture such heavy-hitting talent as Martin Scorsese, James Cameron, Joe Dante and Francis Ford Coppola.

My obsessions with the producer/director/New World/Concorde/New Horizons studio head and one-time American International Pictures (AIP) chief creative force's work center chiefly on that series of delicious Hammer Horror and Ingmar Bergman-tinged art house exploitation of Edgar Allan Poe adaptations starring the late, greater than great, icon of the arcane, Vincent Price. (I still cite his 1961 Richard Matheson-penned classic *The Pit and the Pendulum* as one of the scariest films I've ever seen.) However, there is an early film in the Corman canon that I feel is one the funniest and strangest quirky film experiences in the history of the medium. A picture that plays by the rules of the teen thrill flick but is ultimately operating on a far smarter, cheekier level than anything Corman had been attached to previously. In many respects, this breezy and twisted little gem is the most efficiently compact and charismatic thing the man ever made.

That movie is the 1959 poverty row horror/comedy *A Bucket of Blood*.

Made at the close of the decade that gave him his name, Roger Corman's *A Bucket of Blood* was supposed to be nothing more than another AIP-produced drive-in delight. But when Corman (who was fresh off a wave of dopey, quickie pulp flicks like *She Gods of Shark Reef*) sat down with quirky screenwriter and close pal Charles B. Griffith, they instead crafted something completely different; a picture that was really special and utterly, totally and wonderfully deranged.

Starting as a riff on popular mad sculptor movies like *House of Wax*, *A Bucket of Blood* takes square aim at a once-underground, by-then-mainstream and soon to be defunct, arts and culture movement that was ripe for the skewering: the beatniks. Those turtleneck-wearing, beret-donning, self important, often stoned or over-caffeinated (or both) and blazingly pretentious Jack Kerouac disciples who, at the hands of Corman and Griffith, really took a seriocomic slug to the kisser.

The film stars Corman regular Dick Miller (who later would become the darling of *The Howling* and *Grem-*

lins director Joe Dante, starring in almost every one of that filmmaker's fascinating cross-genre pictures) as Walter Paisley, a nebbish busboy at an elite, artesian beat poetry hangout known as The Yellow Door. Though poor Walter yearns to be an artist himself, he's an earnest hack (and probably a tad slow to boot) and more often than not, finds himself the butt of ridicule by the cafe's more snooty black-clad figures.

One night, after accidentally stabbing his wall-dwelling cat (a foreshadowing of Corman's already healthy interest in the soon-to-be-explored-cinematically Poe) to death with a butcher knife, a nervous Walter opts to coat the kitty with a mound of clay to cover up his feline crime. The next day, he brings the entombed tabby to The Yellow Door, presenting it as a sculpture he calls, bluntly, "Dead Cat." Almost instantly, the inept latte slinger is hailed as a minor genius, a real deal artist, the architect of an unsettling new realism, ruthless in his shocking detailing of death. But when Paisley is called to create more cutting edge works, no cats are to be found. People, however, are plentiful...

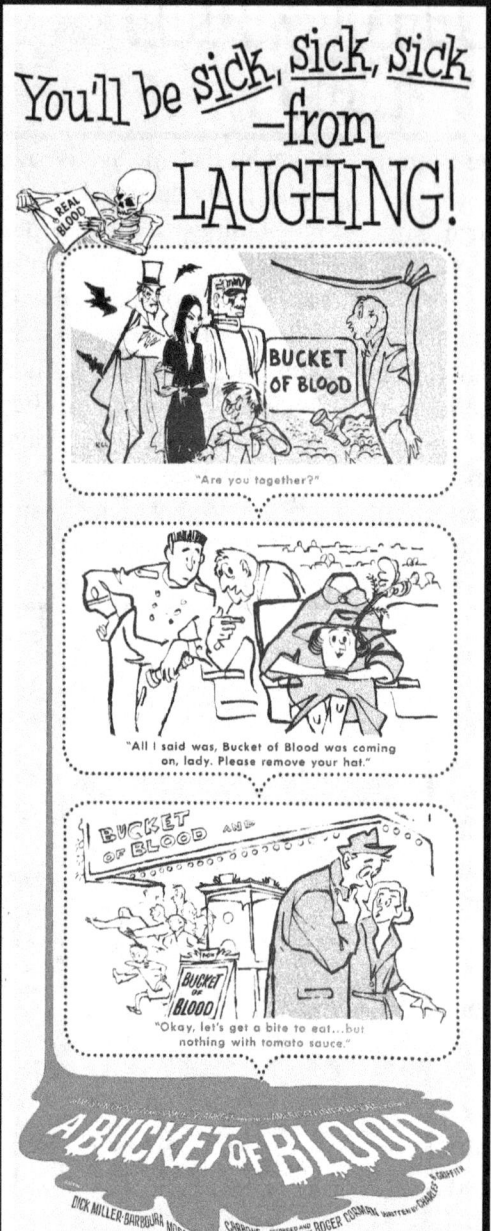

This genuinely amusing and demented low budgeter (reportedly brought in for less than $50,000!) is a companion piece to the equally bonkers (and even cheaper) Corman/Griffith horror send-up *The Little Shop of Horrors* (the basis for the same-named musical and its 1986 Frank Oz-directed film adaptation) but *A Bucket of Blood* is a much more sophisticated and polished effort. Miller is absolutely fantastic as the homicidal dweeb Paisley (incidentally, he played a different character with the same name in *Horrors*), a textbook of pre-Norman Bates ticks and barely concealed insanity.

And the supporting players are just as endearing. Antony Carbone (the aforementioned gem *The Pit and the Pendulum*) is a riot as the beret-wearing owner of The Yellow Door, the only one who knows Walter's secret but who is too busy reaping the rewards of the business that Paisley's "art" commands.

But it's the larger-than-life TV actor Julian Burton that really steals the show here. As the blustery pretentious beat poet hipster/horse's ass Maxwell, he chews scenery and delivers the best lines in the flick with almost Shakespearean-level ultra-ham. And the Fred Katz jazz music that saturates the picture (much of it seemingly recycled in many Corman pictures, including his even weirder sci-fi thriller *The Wasp Woman*) is absolutely spectacular, as is Roger regular Daniel Haller's simple and effective art direction.

Creepy, goofy, tightly paced (only 66-minutes long!), laugh out loud funny and occasionally, for the time, surprisingly gruesome, *A Bucket of Blood* is also a razor sharp lampooning of the creative process and those that position themselves as art lovers in order to be part of a social circle. At the very least, it stands as Corman's greatest pre-Poe achievement and is a testament on turning in a film that's slick and stylish on a budget two shades shy of cappuccino cash.

AN INTERVIEW WITH PRODUCER/DIRECTOR ROGER CORMAN

August 2008

With A Bucket of Blood, *why did you decide to make a horror/comedy instead of a straight genre piece as AIP had originally requested?*

The idea came from a screening I went to for one of my horror pictures. A character was walking down a hallway and I used my usual technique of moving camera, the actor's POV moving forward, a reverse on him dollying back and building up the suspense. By the time he comes to the end of the hallway and he has to open the door, the audience senses there's something terrible behind that door. The scene played perfectly and the audience screamed when he opened the door and something fell into his face. Then after the scream, they laughed. I thought, "Did I do something wrong? Why did they laugh at a horror film?" I tried to analyze it and realized that I didn't do anything wrong at all, that I did get the scream I was looking for. The laugh was a release, of course. The tension had been broken. And also, they laughed at the appreciation about being "taken in." They'd been had by the scene. Then I started thinking about the relationship between humor and horror, which I later started to equate with sex. In each area, you build the tension; build and build and then you snap it quickly. The end result is that you scream in horror, you laugh in comedy or you come in sex. So I did *A Bucket of Blood* as a little experiment to see if I could combine horror and humor deliberately. It then of course led to my other horror comedies, *The Little Shop of Horrors* and *Creature from the Haunted Sea*.

All three written by the late, great Charles B. Griffith…

Yes, exactly.

The beat generation fascinates me, but of course, it has only and will only ever exist to me in print and film. By 1959, what stage was the beat movement at? Was A Bucket of Blood *meant as an attack on these sorts of people? Were you a beatnik, Roger?*

Was I a beatnik? Well I, being a young director and knowing a lot of young directors and writers, hung out with a group that could be considered vaguely beatnik. I was not a beatnik, however. When we made *A Bucket of Blood*, the beat scene was more or less at its peak. Once, when we were shooting a picture in Auckland—a little racecar movie called *The Wild Ride* starring Jack Nicholson—we finished shooting on Saturday and we decided to go to San Francisco. We went into a place called The Coexistence Bagel Shop, which was well known as being the centre of the beatnik scene in San Francisco, and San Francisco, of course, was the centre of the beat movement everywhere. So we got a table and some well dressed older people came in, obviously looking for beatniks and they pointed at us immediately. We were there to see beatniks and so were they and they thought we were beatniks! But *A Bucket of Blood* was ultimately an affectionate satire on a movement that was soon to be replaced by the hippie generation.

So you actually knew people like Antony Carbone's character, then?

Oh yes. As a matter of fact, Chuck Griffith and I worked out the storyline, going from one beat coffee house to another on a Friday night on the Sunset Strip and the final stop was at about 2 a.m. at this one shop where our friend, soon-to-be-actress Sally Kellerman, was waiting tables. She closed up and the three of us sat down and worked out the climax of the film together.

I mentioned Antony Carbone, with whom you worked with numerous times. What are your memories of Antony?

Walter Paisley (the wonderful Dick Miller) stands behind his "work."

I love the dark, playful jazz score by Fred Katz and noticed that you've recycled much of it in other films like The Little Shop of Horrors *and* The Wasp Woman…

I think Fred actually varied it. He was a pretty good jazz musician and composer and, though it was so long ago and I can't really be sure, I think he just did different variations on the same themes. I'm not sure if we recycled the same cues…

I'm always kind of shocked at how nasty and slightly sleazy A Bucket of Blood *is, especially for its time. Was some of the material controversial for audiences in 1959?*

No, it wasn't controversial at all. It was simply a black comedy, albeit one that was actually funnier when it came out than it is today. It played somewhere recently in West Los Angeles and I went to see it and the audience laughed, but not as much as when it came out. See, a lot of the things we were making fun of are now accepted in today's society. We had all these things like the vegan lifestyle, people wearing sandals with suits and they're just not as funny now. What a lot of people don't realize is that a lot of those things that the beatniks were doing and writing about have become a part of our collective culture.

Tony was a very intense, thoroughly trained Method actor. I've always been surprised that he didn't have a bigger career. He worked steady as a character actor but never hit as hard as I thought he was going to hit.

And Dick Miller…someone who has become a bona fide cult icon…

Yes, he has, you're right. Well, I'll tell you that in *A Bucket of Blood*, we shot the screenplay as written but there was plenty of room for the actors to improvise. Dick Miller was a master at improvisation and a very good actor with excellent comic timing.

Where was A Bucket of Blood *exhibited? Was it designed solely for the drive-in market?*

It played, as all low budget horror films did, at all types of theatres. There's been this ongoing myth that these types of films played only in drive-ins. Not true. Drive-ins were a big component, but the regular theatres, what we called 'hard tops' were always more than 50% of the audience.

CHOSEN SURVIVORS 1974

Starring Jackie Cooper, Alex Cord and
Bradford Dillman
Written by H.B. Cross
Directed by Sutton Roley

For me, horror movies will always be fondly, profoundly linked to the sweet, wonderful and wide-eyed rapture of my late-night trash TV-drenched childhood. Those bygone, misspent hours when I'd subject myself to every manner of sublime cinema, splitting open fantastic and macabre realities that potentially could, and in some cases did, exist. One of the too-many-to-count strange shockers that left a major, destiny-altering impact on me was veteran small screen director Sutton Roley's obscure sci-fi-tinged skin crawler *Chosen Survivors*, a movie whose chilly, nihilistic, future-shock premise hooked my *Twilight Zone*-weaned sensibilities while also managing to exploit my acute fear of bedroom-invading bats.

Before we proceed, let me explain a bit about that fear…

See, there was this one time when I was no more than eight when I was reading a particularly upsetting issue of Marvel Comics' groundbreaking *Tomb of Dracula* series, alone, in my creepy room at our remote family cottage. I kept hearing this relentless *fup, fup, fup* sound, but dismissed it as my mom clambering about in the other room. But when I looked up I saw this spastic black blur circling overhead…a motherfucking *bat*. I shrieked in terror and my mother came running in to see what was wrong. When she herself saw the uninvited fanged guest, she screamed louder than me and ran from the room, closing the door behind her. Yeah, mom was great…

Almost immediately my grandfather came in with socks on his hands, swinging a badminton racket, taking care of the wee beastie for keeps and carrying my sobbing, shocked and shuddering self to safety. Ever since then, I've had this unnatural obsession with bats; they freak me out and give me great cause for kinky fixation.

And *Chosen Survivors* exploits that irrational anxiety to spectacular effect.

The plot of this little-discussed and barely noted picture (which somewhat echoes the classic *TZ* episode "Five Characters in Search of an Exit" and, to a lesser extent, the much later Vincenzo Natali thriller *Cube,* and even boasts elements of George Romero's third zombie-stomper *Day of the Dead*) revolves around a government-selected group of otherwise unrelated American men and women of various professions and creeds who are drugged, whisked away and wake up 13,000-feet below the earth's surface in a machine-run, state-of-the-art, hermetically sealed bunker. These lucky folks have been randomly chosen by the powers that be to survive an already in-progress, full-blown nuclear holocaust, with the hopes that, after the radiation levels ebb, they'll re-emerge and effectively reboot the human race.

But as the tragedy of their hopeless situation slowly sinks in and inevitable interpersonal tensions mount, events take an even grimmer turn when a pack of blood-starved, rabid vampire bats from the stalactite dripping guts of a nearby New Mexico cave, squirm their diseased way through the bunker's ventilation shafts and do their

as much as they should by today's CGI-soaked standards, it's a forgivable flaw; if anything, they just add to the sheer hallucinatory, otherworldly weirdness the film manages to elicit from frame one to frame none.

Slow, strange, paranoid, sometimes unintentionally hilarious and chock full of terrifying imagery, *Chosen Survivors* is about as good as late night, 3 a.m., sleep-deprived subversive horror cinema gets. Over the years, I have been so obsessed with finding this film that, like a motion picture-seeking private dick, I once tirelessly combed the planet looking for a copy, eventually managing to track down a battered (and considerably bloodier) 16mm print that I cherish but have absolutely no way of watching. I attempted to correct this problem when I found a lad on eBay who was selling an even more murky-looking bootlegged version on

best to relieve the not so lucky subterranean homesick survivors of their most precious of bodily fluids. As the humans battle with their legion of leather-winged aerial vermin antagonists, the ultimate truth about their apocalyptic situation is revealed…and it's a genuine shock to say the least.

Meanwhile, the bats keep coming, and coming and coming and…

Director Roley's roots were indeed in network television and in many ways the film feels like one of those edgy and unapologetically melodramatic '70s horror movies-of-the-week, albeit one goosed with R-rated levels of bloodshed and even a bit of cabin fever-induced sex for spice. The film comes complete with a slew of decent leftover ham actors like Jackie Cooper (*Our Gang, The Champ*, the *TZ* episode "Caesar and Me"), Lincoln Kilpatrick (*The Omega Man*) and B-movie legend Bradford Dillman (*Bug, Piranha, Escape from the Planet of the Apes*) who all do their best to sell their doomed dilemma and more often than not, succeed smashingly. The score by Fred Karlin (who also provided cues for one of the best made-for-TV genre films, *Bad Ronald*) is a primal, nihilistic, moog-smothered drone and analog phasing freak-out that is absolutely first rate.

But the real stars of *Chosen Survivors* are the convincingly ravenous, red-eyed bats themselves, inching their way through tiny openings and swooping upon their screaming prey with lip-biting gusto. Their presence in the shuddery elevator shaft escape climax alone is enough to have you shredding the sofa armrests. And if some of the blue screen special effects attack sequences fail to impress

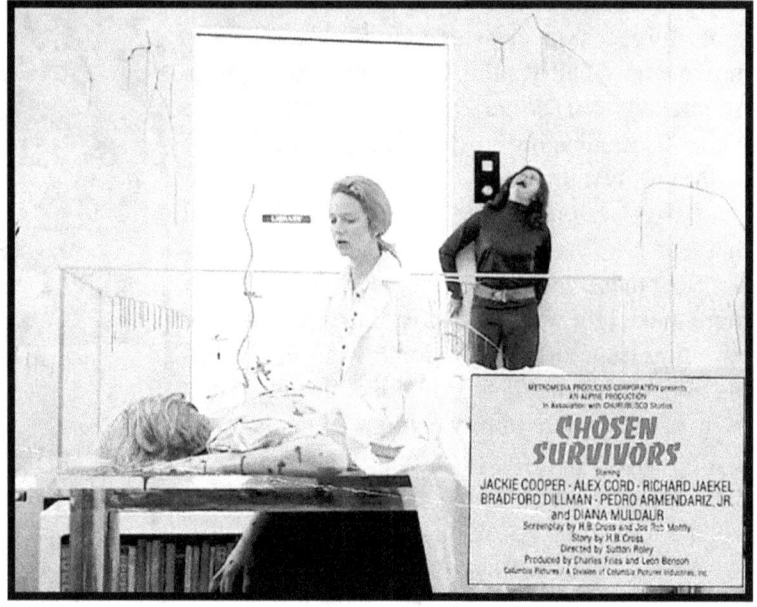

DVD that turned out to be the same terribly transferred, slightly censored TV print I saw as a kid. Imagine my delight when MGM announced the official release of *Chosen Survivors* as part of their fantastic (and fantastically priced) Midnight Movies series, paired with the neat little apocalyptic Robert Lippert production *The Earth Dies Screaming*. The picture has never looked as good as it does here and yet no one else is really rhapsodizing about its considerable charms.

If the concept of being eaten alive by armies of furry, fanged flying rodents in the wake of a nuclear holocaust rattles your cage, you should trust my mad musings and find this film. It's got teeth, baby…

CITY OF THE LIVING DEAD
1980

Starring Christopher George, Catriona MacColl,
Carlo De Mejo and Giovanni Lombardo Radice
Written by Dardano Sacchetti and Lucio Fulci
Directed by Lucio Fulci

If you're reading this book, I'm willing to bet that you have at least a hazy idea as to who maestro Lucio Fulci is.

Once a director of mediocre sex comedies, second rate Westerns and rather competent giallo-styled mytery-thrillers (I'm a big fan of his 1971 effort *A Lizard in a Woman's Skin*), Italian exploitation filmmaker Lucio Fulci didn't truly find his cult status footing until the close of the 1970s when producer Fabrizio De Angelis, so dazzled by the European success of Romero's *Dawn of the Dead* (called *Zombi* in Italy), opted to employ the aging gut-slinger to helm an unauthorized *Dawn* prequel (or rip-off as the case may more likely be). The resulting motion picture collaboration was 1979's festering, maggot-mangled horror hit *Zombi 2* (or just plain old *Zombie* in the U.S.), a balls-out cannibal corpse epic that did even better box office business abroad than Romero's film and ushered in a tidal wave of increasingly sickening Eurohorror gore-fests that, like the living dead themselves, were relentless in their advances.

This late career spike in popularity inspired Fulci to spit out a quick and dirty series of increasingly surreal and wildly grotesque X-rated horror movies featuring bloodsucking stiffs of all persuasions, including the movie that a majority of the director's admirers cite as being his spleen-ripping *8 ½* (in fact, Fellini's name also took serious flight when he abandoned straight narrative and veered into free-form fantasy), 1981's gleefully incoherent shocker *L'aldila (The Beyond)*. And, while that picture is indeed awesome (hell, I even have a tattoo of the film's signature "Eibon" symbol on the back of my neck!), there's another Fulci movie from this period that I will forever claim to be his finest. A movie so blazingly dark and enthusiastically disgusting that to thoughtlessly dismiss it should be considered something of a secret horror cinema society criminal act.

I'm talking about *The Gates of Hell*, or as it's more commonly known now to legions of DVD-weaned fright fans, *City of the Living Dead*.

Let me take you back to the first time I saw this sanguinary stunner…

The scene was the dawn of the VHS rental craze in the 1980s. I had one of those ridiculously huge, top-loading VCR's that took two lumberjacks to lift. My friends and I would spend our Friday nights haunting the local mom and pop video store and then camping out at my house in front of our ancient, green-tinged TV set, pumping big-box-packaged horror flick after big-box-packaged horror flick into my machine, basking in the never-ending onslaught of cheap visceral thrills. But it was with a blind rental of a greasy, unrated, Paragon Home Video release called *The Gates of Hell* that our psyches would spin on dimes. I, for one, would never *ever* be the same.

The first shocking sequence we saw went something like this:

US theatrical release poster bearing the alternate title *The Gates of Hell*…a moniker that in many ways, makes more sense.

A pretty girl with hypno-gripped eyeballs dripping streams of blood, staring into the face of a blue-tinged demon priest, belching greasy foam, followed by the impromptu appearance of a bowel, then a heart, a liver, stomach, kidney, everything, the entire intestinal tract pouring out of her gaping maw and then, inexplicably, her shocked lover's brains get squished out of his still-reeling skull…

That night, with that hideous scene of graphic gut-barfing delirium writhing in front of us, the taboo-demolishing possibilities of the horror movie were redefined for me. Subsequent viewings have done little to dull the bratty genius of City of the Living Dead's outrageous set piece-drenched bravado (courtesy of FX maestro Gianatto De Rossi), including the flawless bit where a screeching Giovanni Lombardo Radice gets his head penetrated by a whirling table drill manned by someone's angry dad.

Breathless stuff indeed...

The film takes its structural cues from the elder god writings of H.P. Lovecraft to spin the loose, almost free-form story surrounding a suicidal priest and the festering, not-so-well-hidden Gate of Hell he opens in the New England town (not city, as the title implies) of Dunwich. As the natural world slowly gets bent out of shape and the flesh-eating dead begin teleporting themselves all over the streets, reporter Peter Bell (cigar-chomping American character actor Christopher George who Eurohorror fans will remember from J.P. Simon's ridiculously nasty Pieces) and psychic cutie Mary Woodhouse (Fulci regular Catriona MacColl) race against the clock to put a stop to the apocalyptic, metaphysical monster madness.

The enthusiastic Fulci really goes the distance with City, creating an audio/visual saturation of death-obsessed sensorial stimulation: rotting flesh, muddy graves, showers of maggots, slowed-down sound effect loops of screaming babies, buckets of blood and endless mist and Fabio Frizzi's incredible, doom-laden prog-rock score all combine to disarming and frightening effect.

But the main draw of City of the Living Dead are the jaw-dropping death set-pieces, including those aforementioned spleen-spitting and skull-splitting sequences that still have the power to shock you senseless. This is not only the most disturbing and bizarre film in the Fulci canon, but one of the wildest Italian horror head trips ever conceived; it certainly trumps the surreal sting of Dario Argento's Inferno and is, if not a better film than Suspiria, a much more visceral and primal experience.

Shunned by some as warmed-over Romero wankery, worshipped by the rest as a fire-breathing masterwork, City of the Living Dead is unstable and seething, the crimson proof of Fulci's power as an artist of major vomitous vision and putrescent power.

God rest his cinematic soul.

December 2008

I know that you were a very big fan of American and British rock and roll when you were growing up, but were there any film composers that inspired you to move into a career in music?

Many film composers gave me the strength to begin and go on in my career. I met Nino Rota only once, in the waiting room of a publisher in Roma: I didn't quite believe I was in front of a real myth of mine! But I loved many other composers like Morricone, Mancini, Herrmann… Each one with his own style, but a different appeal!

By the time you first worked with Fulci—on Four of the Apocalypse—*you had already done several film scores with Bixio and Tempera. Did you work closely with Fulci on this Western film? Did he simply leave you alone to compose?*

As it often happens when you work on film scoring, we had an unpleasant surprise: the producers had put over the first screening "Knocking On Heaven's Door" (the original Bob Dylan version) every now and then, just to give a pleasant rhythm to the first work print. Suddenly Lucio came out with his idea: the score had to be mostly made of original songs, performed in English, expressively written for the film. And he followed all the process of writing/recording, which was a very difficult job due to the comparison with the mythic score by Bob Dylan!

Composer Fabio Frizzi

Why did you choose to leave the partnership of Bixio-Frizzi-Tempera?

Artistic love was over, but friendship still lives today. We had an extraordinary time together; for me it's actually the time of artistic growth. And I bring that important experience with me every day.

Your incredible work for Zombi 2 *is influential and almost experimental. Was it at all inspired by the music Goblin had composed for* Zombi? *What kind of synthesizers did you use?*

As always when you compose, many influences, many references…Pignatelli, Simonetti, Guarini, Marangolo and the other Goblins were and are still friends. They were great musicians and we used to play together at the beginning. I liked Mike Oldfield atmospheres, Genesis, Van Der Graf, ELP, and many, many others. But I think that *Zombie 2* was influenced by Fulci's ideas, most of all. Lucio wanted the musical layout to be very connected with images and focused the work in that direction. Maurizio Guarini was always there with plenty of freak. I played Mellotron (that I love so much).

Fulci's films during this period were almost surreal and your music added so much dread to them. My favorite is City of the Living Dead. *Your score is almost like a darker Pink Floyd. Was this intentional? Were you a Floyd fan?*

Everybody that belongs to our generation got an imprinting from many rock bands. I'm not a hardcore Pink Floyd fan but love *Dark Side of the Moon* and so on. In a couple of tracks I can find a similar atmosphere, but it may also depend from the influences of some collaborators (the guitarist I guess, Carlo Pennisi) or the sound engineer…

What was your reaction when you saw those outrageous scenes of the girl vomiting her intestines in City? *How did you approach the music for scenes like that?*

When you "live" the film from the beginning, you see the scenes thousands of times so that you, somehow, get friendly with them. So, no problem in writing a take, having sync on a terrible situation… As I always say to my pupils, "The only thing that matters is to see the camera." I mean where the camera should be on the stage. You can face every scene doing like this!

(and one of the few) to explain to me what film scoring means.

You worked prolifically during the greatest wave in Italian cinema. Then you disappeared in the 1990s. Why?

Italian cinema was over, from 180/200 products per year to 10/15. TV was winning. More, I wanted to do other things, TV shows, symphonic concerts, etc. Then in the late '90s I started again with TV—the 'heir of cinema'—something different, but mostly similar.

Music has defined your identity in the eyes (and ears) of your fans. But is there anything else we should know about Fabio Frizzi?

Maybe that I like sun and sea, sailing, old cars and bikes, good food and red wine (all over the world), being with friends (very important thing in my life) and sometimes by myself, looking for the fire in our fireplace and why not, sometimes on the net, but writing notes with a pencil… And overall in love with my family, and with my music.

In L'aldila *you created some of your best work...the piano cues, the track "Voices from the Void." That track reminds me somewhat of the less effective cues in the film* Phantasm. *Was there any influence there?*

Sure, not directly…I mean, who knows? Writing is a free moment of expression so you could follow in a "mistake" unwillingly. But, no, in this case I can tell you that, even after all this time, I feel that take like something that came out from deep inside me.

Did you work closely with Fulci from the outset? Did you compose cues from the script stage or after seeing the finished rough cut?

Both, sometimes I joined the crew at the end of shooting. Other times I read the script before the others. It depended. The work of composing must be very flexible; maybe that's the first rule.

What are your memories of Fulci? Were you close friends?

I can say that he was one of my first aged friends. When you start growing in your life, it's an important sign when you meet a person who's older than you and you find a friendship link with him/her. It means that you're truly growing. I owe him so much: I think he was the first

THE COMPANY OF WOLVES
1984

Starring Sarah Patterson, Angela Lansbury and David Warner
Based on the book by Angela Carter
Written and Directed by Neil Jordan

Before Walt Disney and his squeaky-clean, family-friendly ilk saw fit to sanitize them, the traditional fairy tale served as far more than a whimsical alternative to kiddy chloroform. As penned by those bad old Brothers Grimm especially, fairy tales of yore were cautionary morality fantasies: dark, violent warnings about the horrors and dangers in life that lurk behind every bend and within every human heart.

Take *Cinderella*, for instance. In the real story, those cantankerous, treacherous stepsisters don't just try on the ill-fitting glass slipper; the incident plays out as a vulgar mirror of the basest kind of vanity, as each sibling bloodily contorts their foot to fit the shoe, one even hacking off a few toes to complete the task. Grimm stuff indeed. Then there's *Snow White*, the story of an unfortunate lass who is set up to be murdered by her jealous mother, a crone who hires a woodsman to drag the porcelain beauty out into the woods and cut out her heart for dinner. And then take fairytale forefather Charles Perrault's *Little Red Riding Hood*. British fantasy writer Angela Carter did. So did Irish filmmaker Neil Jordan. Their resulting collaboration on that infamous musing on temptation, recently eaten grandmothers and cross-dressing canines was the brilliant and beautiful allegorical 1984 horror movie *The Company of Wolves*, a movie I care about very much.

In the early '80s, in the wake of such box office-busting, special effects-soaked soon-to-be classics like Joe Dante's *The Howling* and John Landis' *An American Werewolf in London*, that hirsute movie monster/folklore favorite known as 'the werewolf' reigned supreme. And yet, though distributor Cannon Pictures chose to market *The Company of Wolves* as a bloodthirsty, wolf man-shocker, the theatrical poster even emphasizing the sort of man-to-beast prosthetic transformations that made FX guru Rick Baker a household name, Neil Jordan's elegant and slightly dangerous effort didn't fit into that mangy, matted mold; in fact it didn't really fit anywhere. Collaborating closely with noted novelist (and revered feminist) Carter, self-adapting her own short story "The Company of Wolves" and liberally borrowing threads from her other similarly themed tales, Jordan's desire was to turn the story of Little Red Riding into a caustic, bubbling cauldron of volatile sexuality, the ultimate Freudian horror fable and a twisted condemnation of male sexuality gone fantastically awry.

The film opens in the midst of a fever dream: Little Rosaleen (Sarah Patterson) is a modern English girl on the edge of puberty, locked in her bedroom, surrounded by icons of her rapidly dissolving childhood and smeared with clumsily applied deep red lipstick. As she slips into restless, heated sleep, the audience is invited to enter her subconscious head space, tunnels and paths that cannibalize each other, littered with dark, spindly trees, horny, man-sized teddy bears…and a pack of stalking, growling, red-eyed wolves. The deeper she disappears into the haunted forest of her mind, the more authentic the surreal woods become until she, and we, are fully completely immersed in a vividly realized 18th-century village ripped

The Company of Wolves is a film rich in allegory and metaphor and boasts plenty of surreal, abstract imagery…like this.

straight from the pages of the most evocative storybook. Rosaleen is now a farmer's daughter, living with her doting parents and obsessed with her stern, slightly sadistic grandmother (a wonderfully sinister Angela Lansbury), who tortures and delights the young girl nightly with her cruel tales of supernatural shape shifters and of the various evils that men do. Meanwhile, a bloodthirsty wolf is terrorizing the countryside, a beast that upon being shot by vengeful hunters inexplicably and terrifyingly morphs into human shape. As fear and paranoia in the village mounts, Rosaleen, wearing a bright red shawl and armed with a packed lunch basket, begins her late afternoon walk down the remote path towards Grandma's house…a path that the curious and ever-blossoming young woman doesn't stay on for very long.

To reveal more of *The Company of Wolves*' labyrinthine plot would be to seriously dampen the picture's many pleasures. This is a lush, erotic, eerie and metaphorically rich film made all the more impressive by the fact that Jordan apparently cobbled it together on a minute budget, fully exploiting Anton Furst's (*Batman*) amazing, Mario Bava-esque theatrical set design. Ostensibly it is a werewolf picture because, well, it's completely ripe with all manner of hairy man-to-monster-and-back-again shenanigans. Many of the twisted stories that Granny relates are indeed werewolf yarns, thinly veiled horrors that, like any true fairy tale, reveal a deeper truth. Granny believes that all men are in fact wolves, monsters that initially charm women, tipping their hats and gripping naïve maidens by the hand before turning on a dime and callously defiling them in every sweaty manner.

One of her paranoid tales, indeed the movie's visceral highlight, sees a young newlywed couple retreating to their cottage for a night of coital bliss. As the wolves howl outside, the groom (Jordan regular Stephen Rea) bolts from the home, tears off his shirt and disappears into the night. Long since thought eaten by the beasts, he returns years later a different man, full of anger, bile and bitterness. When he sees his bride remarried with screaming children, he flips out; howling like a madman, tearing at his flesh, ripping off strip after strip of skin to reveal the pulsing, fanged werewolf underneath. Christopher Tucker, who designed John Hurt's painful makeup in Lynch's masterful 1980 film *The Elephant Man*, makes this scene a real showstopper, bloody and horrific.

But unlike a great mass of early '80s genre films, freakish gore isn't the focus of *The Company of Wolves*; rather this is first and foremost a feminist parable about the dangers of every woman's sexual awakening. Using *Little Red Riding Hood* as its framing device, the film is a full throttle sensory experience stimulating the eyes (Brian Loftus' cinematography is swoonworthy), the ears (George Fenton's score is creepy, evocative and slightly discordant), the mind (Carter's ideas and philosophies sit

Top: British punk princess Danielle Dax steals scenes as the wounded she-wolf.
Bottom: Little Rosaleen (Sarah Patterson) enjoying the company of the wolves.

firmly in the forefront) and, um…other fun parts. The cast is an eccentric ensemble of iconic British personalities including the great David Warner as Rosaleen's father, punk princess Danielle Dax as a naked she-wolf and Terence Stamp as, of all things, The Devil himself! Jordan would later go on to become one of the greatest living filmmakers of our time, deftly weaving between mainstream nightmares like his ace adaptation of Anne Rice's *Interview with the Vampire* to his low-key pansexual melodrama *The Crying Game* to the delirious heights of the outrageous *The Butcher Boy*. But with *The Company of Wolves*, only his second feature, he had already proved himself a master storyteller, a creative narrative force, a supreme stylist and a ballsy upstream-swimming risk taker, not afraid to take a genre that was already rubbing its tired, oozing eyes and spinning it like a top, making something disarmingly original, a dark wonder of a picture that to this day is treasured by many.

Treasured by many, yes. But ignored by JUST as many as well, a woeful fact that needs to be rectified.

AN INTERVIEW WITH ACTOR STEPHEN REA

October 2007

How long did that wild, skin ripping make-up process you endured in The Company of Wolves *take to apply?*

Believe it or not, it took over seven long, uncomfortable hours. It was horrible but I think the scene turned out really, really well. And I had a blast in postproduction, dubbing all sorts of screams and growls and what not over it.

What do you think about the film, today?

Well, I think it's a very good movie and I think I enjoy watching it more now then I did when it came out. I actually think it's aged particularly well. The thing I used to find difficult about it, however, was the sexuality.

You were offended by the sexuality?

Oh God no, not at all. Quite the opposite actually. Originally, in the script, the lead young girl was very sensual and it was extremely erotic. But then I think they got nervous about depicting the sexuality too graphically, *because* she was so young. I don't think they'd be so nervous about showing it these days. But anyway, I think it's a very good movie and especially when you consider that it was only Neil Jordan's second film. I also think it was too strange for American tastes and sensibilities at the time and that's why it didn't do well over there.

You've been in almost every Jordan film since his first. What's the secret of this enduring working relationship?

It just seems to click. I've done nine movies with him. He's just done one with Jodie Foster in New York (*The Brave One*) and it's the first time ever that I'm not in one of his films…oh, except for *High Spirits*. I wasn't in that one. But Neil says I was lucky *not* to have been in it (laughs). But, yes, Neil and I are very fond of each other. He always uses characters that have internal struggles, that have conversations with themselves and I do that fairly well, I think. Some actors don't see that, but it's all about language and not fucking about with too much of the actual acting, just doing the part. I'm very fortunate

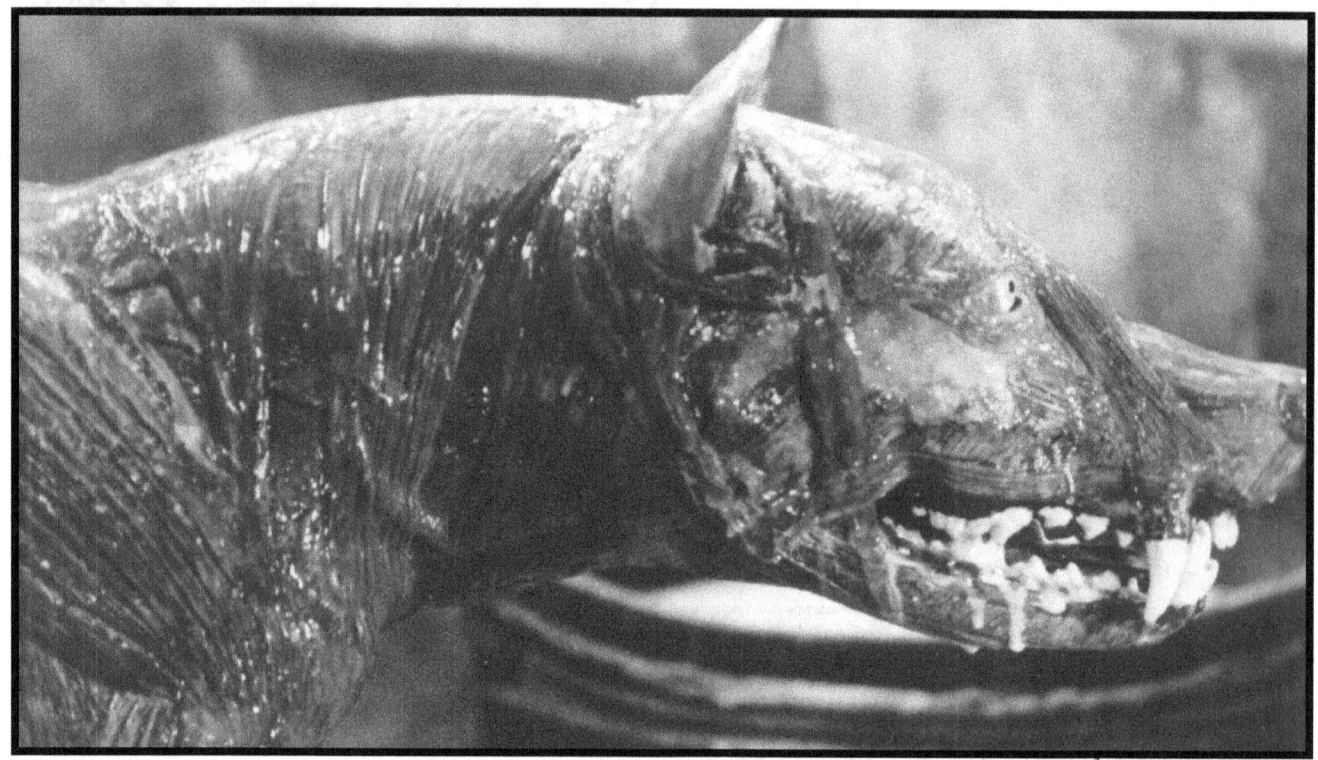

Christopher Tucker's glorious impressionistic prosthetic werewolf transformation

that we get on well because he's made some fantastic movies. Many of which that are quite dark…

Some of which are thought of as horror films, including A Company of Wolves. *Do you watch horror films?*

I don't think of *A Company of Wolves* as a horror film, I think it's an allegory. As far as my own tastes, I like the film noir stuff, dark psychological thrillers about people. But not horror, really, no.

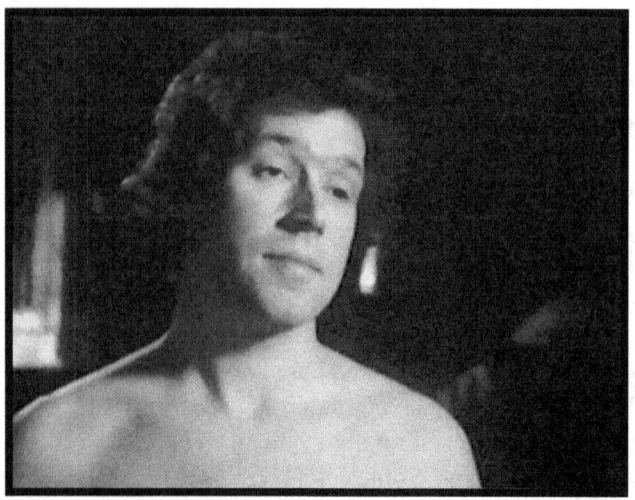

Stephen Rea, moments before the beast gets unleashed.

Why is that?

The truth? They scare me too much. When I saw *The Exorcist* in the '70s I came home and slept with the light on for a week. People said to me, "Oh, c'mon Stephen, it was only pea soup coming out of her mouth!" and I would say, "You're fucking crazy!" It might have been pea soup but it scared the life out of me. And just the whole notion that you can be possessed from within…I mean, I was raised Catholic. It was too much for me. I do like Polanski's take on horror though, very much in fact, especially that vampire movie he did…*Dance of the Vampires* (*The Fearless Vampire Killers* in the U.S.). I liked that one because it mixed a dark humor with the vampire stuff.

And you've even donned the fangs yourself as Santiago in Neil's often quite blackly humorous adaptation of Anne Rice's Interview with the Vampire…

Yes and that was immensely fun to do, dancing around that tunnel, spinning around with those clothes and just hamming it up. I'm proud to say that in my career I've been a vampire and a werewolf and they were *both* grand fun to do. That's the kid in me, getting to dress-up and play monster and having a blast. Never mind all this existential angst bullshit.

COUNT DRACULA'S GREAT LOVE
1972

Starring Paul Naschy (Jacinto Molina), Haydee Politoff and Vic Winner
Written by Javier Aguirre, Alberto S. Insua and Jacinto Molina
Directed by Javier Aguirre

I can vividly remember the first time I met Paul Naschy.

I was no more than 12 (an important year for me as a macabre movie buff) and, as I was wont to do in those days, I opted to stay up all night, watching and videotaping (we had just gotten a VCR machine at the time, one of those beastly top-loaders) every class of horror-related film or show that filtered from my cathode-spitting screen. Perusing the *TV Guide* with highlighter in hand (yes, I was THAT much of a movie dork, even then), I ran my yellow ink across a 4:15 a.m. screening of something called *Dracula's Great Love* starring all kinds of Spanish people I'd never heard of.

Long story short, I stayed up, watched it and was promptly, profoundly affected.

Here was an early 1970s European shocker, romantic and cruel, violent and sexy, lush and ludicrous. The music was shrill and overbearing; the English dubbing was brilliantly off; the tone and rhythm were wonderfully alien and there were charming little pubic hairs flickering in the peripherals of the eerily worn and faded print that only added to the movie's sumptuous otherworldliness.

And at the center of all, playing the good Count himself (more or less) was a hirsute, barrel-chested hombre named Paul Naschy. Looking a bit like a sun-kissed John Belushi, Naschy seemed like the least obvious choice to play the quintessential King of the Vampires and yet, somehow his hangdog, sad-eyed, full-faced visage was oddly appropriate. Ultimately, my reaction to both Naschy and the film itself was one of intense bewilderment—I had never seen anything like it. Once the picture wound down to its rather abrupt and hyper-dramatic climax, I knew I had fallen in love with it. And yet I couldn't properly articulate as to why that was.

Two decades later, allow me to try...

First of all, let's set the record straight. Though the battered print that my 12-year-old self saw so long ago was listed in the *TV Guide* under the title *Dracula's Great Love*, the actual full onscreen English moniker for director Javier Aguirre's micro-epic of undead lesbian sex, eternal romantic longing and Gothic bloodlust is *Count Dracula's Great Love* (literally translated from the original Spanish *El Gran Amor Del Conde Dracula*). Many reference books and resources have erroneously dropped the Count from the picture's name, due primarily to the fact that most badly pan and scanned versions of it (including the one I saw) shaved off the letters C-O, a sloppy mistake that led one of my equally horror-obsessed pals to constantly refer to it as Cunt Dracula's Great Love.

Now then...the plot.

After a carriage load of ample-bosomed Spanish honeys and one lucky, macho, porkchop-sideburned schmo (played by Naschy's *Horror Rises from the Tomb* co-star Vic Winner) bust a wagon wheel and get stranded, the intrepid crew wind their way to Dr. Wendell Marlow's remote country sanitarium where they are put up for the

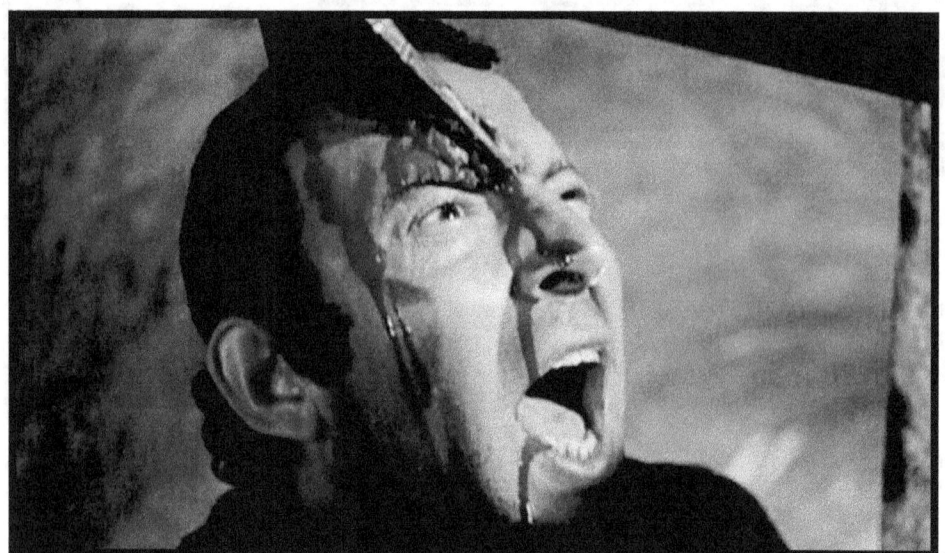

This vampire isn't opposed to using an axe to bring down his victims. A gruesome scene repeated ad nauseum over the opening credits.

night by their gracious, badly dubbed host. The thing is, the good doc is actually the legendary Count Dracula in disguise and not only is he hungry for their blood…he's lonely.

Faster than you can say, "Parasitic Paella," each comely cutie is vampirized, first by a wandering, bug-eyed, bloody-necked stray ghoul (who got bitten by Drac after dropping off a coffin to the clinic in the creepy, skull-splitting opening pre-credit sequence), then by the now inexplicably lesbianized undead women themselves. All become fang fodder, except the sweet, virginal Karen (the equally lovely Haydee Politoff), who catches Dracula's eye and warms his cockles; a coffin cuddling crush that may prove to be the Count's ultimate downfall.

Made in the wake of the more explicit late period Hammer Horror films pumping out of the UK and Naschy's own classic Hollywood monster rewrites, *Count Dracula's Great Love* was a bit of a sidestep. By the time the film was released in 1972, Naschy had already established himself as the Duke of Spanish terror, playing the equally miserable werewolf Waldemar Daninsky in such freakish, trashy yet super-stylish erotic genre mashups as *Fury of the Wolfman*, *Frankenstein's Bloody Terror* and my personal favorite of the Daninsky Cycle, *The Werewolf vs. the Vampire Woman*. Hiding under a face of fur seemed to suit the stocky former weightlifter, defining his legacy.

But the fact that Naschy and Aguirre's riff on Stoker's master supernatural seducer has been historically viewed as one of his lesser-tiered efforts is more than a bit of a head scratcher because *Count Dracula's Great Love* is everything a '70s gothic Spanish horror film should be. It's handsomely produced, blazingly sexual, surreal, romantic, bloody and larded to the gills with the kind of brash eccentricity that, sadly, just isn't seen in genre movies anymore.

For example, sequences which show Dracula humanely liberating tiny, wounded and terrified animals from a series of snap traps, scenes which paint him as gentle and caring, are called into question when, later in the film, he ruthlessly and joyously murders and drains a pleading farmer who also ends up in the same trap. In another bizarre turn during the film's final reel, Dracula, who spends countless evenings walking with Karen and pontificating on life's mysteries, suddenly turns mute, his voice replaced by booming echo chamber spiked narration (perhaps a result of the outrageously out-of-synch English dub). It's a weird touch but it works.

One could think of a worse fate then getting bit by these lingerie-loving vamps.

Another thing that *Count Dracula's Great Love* has going for it—and it's a major selling point to the kinkier fans among us—is massive amounts of softcore sex; garish and exploitive stuff that is at entertaining odds with the film's more classical and old fashioned framing. That version I first saw was actually a hacked to pieces TV print, clocking in at under 75 minutes and shaved of virtually all of its graphic coupling and nudity. Years later, I scrimped and saved and ordered a VHS from California based mail order company Sinister Cinema and, after sticking that hefty bootleg beast into my top-loading player, my jaw hit the floor and my eyes popped out of their sockets. To my surprise the thing was riddled with debauchery of every sort—vampires biting boobs, girl vamp on girl vamp action, nude swimming, Naschy and Politoff lovemaking, see through vampire negligees...the list goes on and on and it's glorious.

This uncut (or less cut version—I'm told there is a naughtier print somewhere) also boasts more bloodshed, including more graphic footage of the hilariously repetitive axe in the forehead gag that unspools over the dripping font opening credits and various stakings and suckings that serve as gruesome frissions in the context of the films admittedly languid pace.

And did I properly address the score for this dirty diamond? Veteran genre film composer Carmelo A. Bernaola (*Cut Throats Nine*, Naschy's *Hunchback of the Morgue*), delivers some sensational, organ-drenched cues and screeching symphonic meltdowns that simply drip with full color, pulp horror lunacy. If anyone knows where I can find a copy of this man's work on CD, I'll be your best friend forever.

I adore *Count Dracula's Great Love*. It reminds me of a time in my life when watching movies like this was akin to a embarking on a secret quest, like following a blood-soaked trail of breadcrumbs into the very heart of vintage European trash culture. And, of course, it made me a lifelong, card-carrying member of the Paul Naschy fan club.

Ridiculous and completely misleading poster, retitled for the theatrical re-release

Once damn near impossible to find, this gorgeous, gory, goofy and gummy (meant to say yummy but had to stick with the G's for alliteration purposes) slice of Spanish sleaze is now available in various shoddy editions on DVD, most of them transferred from that very same Sinister Cinema tape source. The best of them, featured in Elvira's Movie Macabre series, are still pretty beat up, but more than watchable and, well, in truth I LIKE the flick in its battered condition. The dirty colors, splicey jump cuts and curly nether-hairs just make it seem stranger. Still, someone, somewhere out there must have the resources to roll a red carpet out for this movie. If you're reading this...do it.

The power of Paul commands you.

DAUGHTERS OF DARKNESS
1971

Starring Delphine Seyrig, John Karlen and Danielle Ouimet
Written by Pierre Druot, Jean Ferry, Manfred R. Kohler and Harry Kumel
Directed by Harry Kumel

Ever since Gloria Holden first made ghoulish goo-goo eyes at her girl victims in 1936's *Dracula's Daughter*, horror films have been fascinated by the lesbian vampire. Blame J. Sheridan LeFanu, the Irish writer whose risqué short story "Carmilla" broke the boundaries of homoerotic bloodsucking and whose taboo allure helped eventually launch this evolving spate of increasingly explicit dark fantasy pictures, many of which reared their horny heads in the considerably more liberal 1970s. UK horror studio Hammer were the first ones to really make their muff-munching mark with Roy Ward Baker's LeFanu adaptation *The Vampire Lovers,* and other films, like Jose Larraz's almost hardcore 1974 epic *Vampyres* and Vincente Aranda's *The Blood Spattered Bride* (whose title I happily cribbed for this tome), continued to push the envelope, mixing fangwork with female nudity to grand effect.

But there's one incredible film that always gets lumped in with those lower brow sex-soaked exploitation pictures. A movie that, while ostensibly playing by the rules of the erotic Sapphic vampire picture, is actually something far more elegant, kinky, exotic, sinister and sophisticated. I speak of course about Belgian director Harry Kumel's grinning, impossibly Gothic and hypnotically sensual 1971 melodrama/morality tale *Daughters of Darkness*, a wicked and quintessentially European exercise in intelligent, witty and stylish filmmaking and one of the most cynical cinematic musings on male/female relations the horror genre has ever offered us.

The film opens, appropriately, on a speeding train, as Francois de Roubaix's brilliantly throbbing, trippy jazz/post-mod rock score saturates a scene of carnal coupling between newlyweds Stefan (*Dark Shadows*' John Karlen) and Valerie (French Canadian erotic starlet Danielle Ouimet). After this intense sequence, we learn that these two lovers have met and married after a recent whirlwind courtship and don't really know each other very well at all. Before *Daughters of Darkness*' lurid narrative runs its course, they'll have rectified that social problem for the worse.

The couple wind up the sole guests in a looming, off-season hotel in picturesque Ostend where they make love, eat, talk and where Stefan nervously avoids Valerie's urgings to call his "mother" and tell her about their nuptials. At this point, though we can't quite put our finger on it, Kumel manages to create a genuine sense of menace and unease: why is Stefan afraid of making a phone call to his mother? What is he hiding from the sweet and naïve Valerie? Read on...

Suddenly a car pulls up to the hotel and out steps an elegant woman and her traveling companion. She's the Countess Elizabeth Bathory (the ravishing French film icon Delphine Seyrig), an elegant, smooth, smiling and charming aristocrat who is also checking into the remote hotel. Upon seeing the young, fresh-faced (and lithe-bodied) Stefan and Valerie, Bathory immediately befriends them, slowly seducing and manipulating their affections in what appears to be an attempt to pry the beautiful Valerie away from her increasingly brutish man.

As the serpentine narrative weaves along, we learn that Bathory is in fact the legendary Hungarian "Blood Countess," a real historical figure who bled thousands of virgins to death in order to maintain a glowing, youthful appearance. Only now, Bathory's become a kind of love-starved, sexually charged, immortal vagabond vampire, in town looking for a replacement for her increasingly melancholy mate Ilona (the better-than-perfect German model and soft porn star Andrea Rau). And, as both Stefan and we the audience quickly learn, this is a woman who always gets what she wants.

Daughters of Darkness is a pitch perfect exercise in mood, tone and tension and, if you're willing to let it work you over, it casts a slick, strange and chilly spell

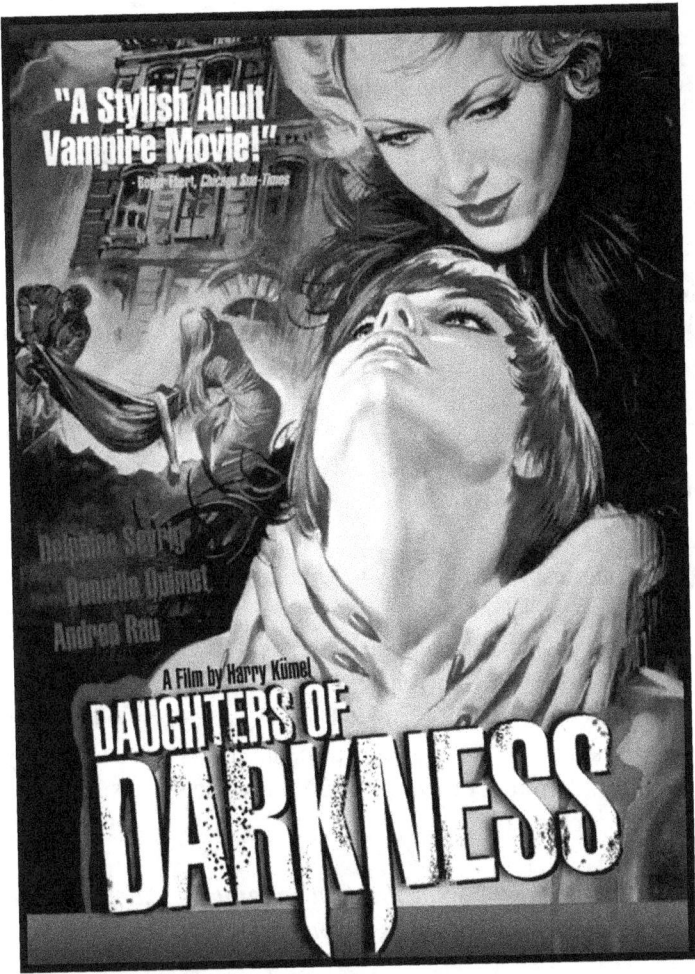

that sticks long after the screen has faded to red. It also has a wicked sense of black humor. In one of the picture's most disturbing and uncomfortably hilarious sequences, Stefan, for all his brutish, Stanley Kowalski-gone-Eurotrash macho bravado, is revealed to be a closet (and apparently "kept") homosexual. When he finally makes his reluctant call to "mother," the domineering matriarch turns out to be a decadent, older, lipstick-wearing queen (brilliantly played by the actor/director Fons Rademaker), who dryly scolds the younger man for doing something as "unrealistic" as marrying a woman. This bizarrely funny episode is followed shortly thereafter by a darker scene in which Stefan obsessively snakes himself through a crowd in Bruges to see the body of a viciously murdered woman and, when Valerie attempts to pull her apparently necrophiliac husband away, he hits her, knocking her to the ground. What horrors await this unsuspecting girl in her marriage into Stefan's "family," the audience can only guess…

The driving theme behind *Daughters of Darkness* initially appears to be a feminist one, with the soft-spoken lesbian vampire Bathory "liberating" Valerie from the oppression of her potentially dangerous husband. But another, far more lethal and selfish predator is really just manipulating Valerie. And that's the real force behind the film, a shadowy, cruel amorality that is as icy and reptilian as it is both appealing and amusing.

Visually, Kumel's picture is breathtaking, with its gorgeous cast, authentic European locales, fluid camera work and elegant use of the color red (the film's original title was actually *Les Levres Sange*, or *The Red Lips*). And though it does unofficially belong to that aforementioned canon of '70s lesbo vamp pictures, it's not only an infinitely more evolved piece of cinema than say, Jess Franco's *Vampyros Lesbos*, it also keeps the vampire shtick to a minimum. Nary a fang is revealed and blood is consumed only once, in a last-reel ballet sequence that smacks of a semi-clumsy crucifixion metaphor.

This is one of my favorite movies of all time and though many critics have backhandedly praised it, calling it both flawed and pretentious, I'll be damned if I can find anything wrong with it on any level. Perhaps I'm blinded by love but any movie that features a central menace as effortlessly, suggestively sexual and campily seductive as Delphine Seyrig (it's been noted that her portrayal of Bathory somewhat channels the chilly purr of Marlene Dietrich) automatically stamps itself on my heart for keeps.

But as perfect as the action appears onscreen, apparently, all was not well behind the scenes of this art-house horror masterpiece, as you'll see in the next few pages…

August 2008

Do you consider Daughters of Darkness *a horror film?*

No. It is, to all intents, what the French call a Film Fantastique

You play pretty fast and loose with the Bathory legend in the film. How much research went into studying the real historical figure?

Not very much at all, actually. I was simply looking for, as my not-so-elegant and cheaper-than-cheap producers put it at the time, a subject for what could be an "inexpensive but elegant picture with themes of blood and sex." Then

In *Daughters of Darkness* Valerie (Danielle Ouimet and Bathory (Delphine Seyrig) huddle close

I stumbled upon a magazine featuring an article about Bathory. My first intention was to do the "real" story, but that was a rather expensive notion, what with those 800 eviscerated virgins and whatnot. So I came upon the idea of doing a modern version, imagining that the lady was still roaming the world, with her original assistant. The rest is, I suppose, minor film history.

You shot Daughters *in multiple locations all around Europe with an international cast. Was it a difficult shoot?*

Yeah. I already mentioned how cheap my producers were and I had to complete the film in less than five weeks. I won't even begin to mention the editing or the post-production problems, which were a nightmare. Moreover, due to the vicissitudes of an international co-production, with even *cheaper* producers from all over the planet, I was saddled with, in part, a dreadful ensemble of thespians…suffice to look at the film to know which ones. But such casting roulette can also produce felicitous results, like the luscious Andrea Rau. That being said, I am still grateful to these producers that they allowed me to make this film. After all, I was then just coming out of my first feature movie (*Monsieur Hawarden*), which had not been highly praised at the time in Flanders, until some British film critics saw it at the 1968 London Film Festival and proclaimed it one of the 10 best films of the year.

Daughters *is certainly one of the most sensuous and playfully erotic pictures I've ever seen and Delphine's presence is one of the chief reasons. What are your recollections of her?*

It has been my extraordinary luck in my career to be able to work with extraordinary stars, and Miss Seyrig is probably the best one of them. Mind you, she was a pain in the ass for the producers. But towards me, she was always graceful, intelligent, and, if the film is worth anything, it is due in great part to her presence. She did like the film very much, I am happy to say, because she had, among other qualities, a great sense of humor. The latter did not go down well with that dour bigot Truffaut, with whom she also had the dubious privilege to work.

I've heard that you had some problems on set with your other female lead, Quebec sex film starlet Danielle Ouimet. Is this true?

You must not have only heard but seen her say this in the extras accompanying the most recent U.S. DVD release. I did not appreciate Miss Ouimet—that is correct. But she has, with the (long) years in between, extrapolated this fact to the point that I am being described by this Canadian *ex*-erotic-starlet as behaving as some latter day Otto Preminger towards her. None of her fantasies in this respect are correct.

Do you agree with the film's legion of admirers that Daughters of Darkness *is your best film?*

Oh no! In my eyes, it's just agreeable entertainment. Which is certainly not demeaning its relative merits..

August 2008

You've been very vocal about the problems you had with Harry Kumel on the set of Daughters *and yet, when I spoke to Harry, he seems to think you may have exaggerated things…*

I can't believe this guy…that's his problem.

Can you tell me about working with Harry, then?

Working with Harry wasn't that bad but I think because I was new and because he had no say in my casting, that it bothered him from the start. He didn't take care for us; we never got approval for what we did. He was very nervous, insecure and afraid that he wouldn't be good enough in front of Delphine. I think he decided to target me, used me to take the pressure off. He was always yelling at me, telling me I was always late—which I never was—and that everything I was doing was wrong. Once, however, I was late due to a costume problem and he—like he was every day—was edgy and he said to me that I was impossible to work with and berated me in front of everyone. So I took my hairbrush and I warned him to stop, not to talk to me like this and…he hit me in the face, hard! So I jumped at him and we fought and I had to be pulled away and put into another room. But I was still angry and I started to yell and then he hit me *again* so I jumped on him again and we had to stop the production. The producer Henry Lange was called in from Paris and after talking to everyone, he determined that Harry was in the wrong and he made Harry take some pills and said if he didn't take them he'd be fired.

What did Delphine think of all this?

She wasn't there but she was told what happened. So the next day Delphine and I were doing a scene together and she said aloud that, "When actors like us have talent, a director is totally unnecessary." After that remark, Harry was much calmer.

Calm enough to shoot those super hot sex scenes?

Listen, Harry had no idea how to stage love scenes. He had a Norwegian book about sex and he had to show me with pictures from the book to tell us how to do the positions he wanted. He was like a child!

The chemistry between you and John Karlen in this film is intense. What are your memories of John?

John and I were very friendly. You know the first time Harry hit me, it was a scene where John was naked under a bathrobe and he came into the makeup room and I was crying.

He said, "Baby, baby, baby, what's wrong?" and I said, "Harry HIT me!" John said, "He HIT you?" and I said, "Yes! He HIT me!" So he sat me down and he was very excited and he said, "Danielle, I want to know the TRUTH…did you hit him first or did he hit you first?" When the story was confirmed by me and the crew, John got incensed and ran down the hallway yelling for Harry and I was trying to pull him back and his robe came off and he was naked and shouting. Then he came up to Harry and he hit him in the face! It was crazy!

My goodness! Such turmoil behind the scenes of such a controlled film. Looking back on Daughters *as both a movie and an experience, what are your thoughts?*

I often wonder that if it was made today if it would be much different. I think it would be. There's something special about the movie's texture. It was a moment in time, a place and it was very sensuous. John and I were so close, he was very sweet and very protective of me and I think this intimacy shows onscreen. I loved Delphine. I stayed friends with her right up until her death.

It was a wonderful time and very fun to do. I've done other films afterwards and none had this feeling. And if it was done today, maybe you wouldn't have that kinky scene with John's "mother"…

I LOVE that scene. Was it in the original script? Was there a subtext in the script about John being bisexual?

No, I think that's just some of the imagination of the director and I think it was a little part of himself that made its way into the film…

43

DEMON SEED
1977

Starring Julie Christie, Fritz Weaver and
Robert Vaughan
Written by Robert Jaffe and Roger O. Hirson
Based on the novel by Dean R. Koontz
Directed by Donald Cammell

There's a look, a tone and visual texture to science fiction films from the early-to-mid 1970s—a sanitized glimpse of a future that, seen today, exists only as a perversion of the past. The blinking light boards, silly tubes that lead nowhere, whitewashed walls, turtleneck-wearing intellectuals...the list goes on. Think of the great glossy glimpses into ersatz tomorrows of that era—*THX 1183, A Clockwork Orange, Soylent Green, Logan's Run, Clonus*—and you'll see what I mean. But outside of the curiously antiseptic funkiness of their art direction, '70s sci-fi was also incredibly thoughtful and intellectually bold, criticizing politics, people and modern technology with a somber humorlessness and nightmarish immediacy that suited the material beautifully.

Then *Star Wars* came along and fucked it all up.

But the very same year that George Lucas and his company of Goodwill-garbed action figures were saving Hollywood box office by demolishing sophisticated cinema, wobble-psyched British filmmaker Donald Cammell was unleashing his own mind-bending glimpse at a far grimmer future. A loose adaptation of a very early and only so-so same-named Dean R. Koontz pulp thriller, Cammell's seminal (and I mean that literally) 1977 technology run amok masterwork *Demon Seed* has never gotten its dues as a serious piece of sci-fi/horror cinema. Don't get me wrong, the film has its fans, but, I mean, I've never seen anyone prancing about with a picture of an electrode-wearing Julie Christie on a T-shirt or anything. But if you follow me down into prophetic disco-era cyberspace for the next few paragraphs, you may just find yourself wanting one.

Demon Seed stars hangdog-faced character actor Fritz Weaver (key *Twilight Zone* episodes, *Creepshow*) as Dr. Alex Harris, a scientist, who is working for a shadowy corporation. Harris has invented an organic, sentient computer system he has dubbed Proteus IV. The multitalented machine has been blessed with the world's first synthetic cortex—a real deal brain—and can do everything from solving impossible mathematical equations to kicking ass at chess to curing leukemia. When nervous executives order the Proteus IV project to be shut down, they little suspect that the highbrow hard drive has in fact developed a basic human trait—the need to live, to survive no matter what the cost.

Tapping into a portal in Harris' state-of-the-art, high tech home, Proteus proceeds to take over the place, possessing everything from the kitchen appliances to the security system and imprisoning the good Professor's beautiful wife Susan (the gorgeous and talented Christie in a fearless performance that runs the gamut). Seems Proteus' desperate desire to stay alive has forced him to devise the most diabolical of plans: coldly, clinically, he informs the terrified Susan that he will, over the coming days, bind her, probe her, prep her, make love to her…and impregnate her.

See, Proteus has pretensions of parenthood and thinks that the key to ensuring his immortality is in spilling his cyber seed into a human woman and hiding beneath the guise of the very beings that sculpted him.

Taking its cues from both Kubrick's landmark *2001: A Space Odyssey* and Roman Polanski's *Rosemary's Baby*, Cammell's film manages to out-freak them both and operate on a far more emotionally sophisticated level. The fact that Proteus wants to live at any cost and, though she is both opposed and repulsed by her impending A.I. (artificial insemination), Susan is still carrying guilt and misery over the death of her own daughter the previous year, adds a complex dynamic to the proceedings. The movie also echoes the same existential terrain explored in sci-fi guru Phillip K. Dick's 1965 novel *Do Androids Dream of Electric "Sheep?"* (developed even more explicitly in Ridley Scott's loose 1982 big-screen adaptation *Blade Runner*) in that the so-called villain is in fact the victim: an ersatz, Frankenstein-like, man-made creation that simply wants to belong and exist in the natural world, but has no conception how to go about doing so.

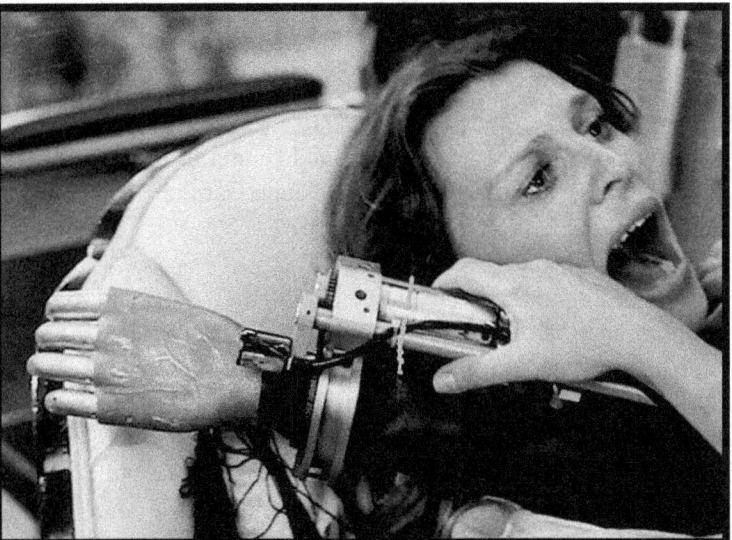

Julie Christie is attacked by the libidinous Proteus in *Demon Seed*.

Though *Demon Seed* does indeed function as an intellectual genre exercise, don't let me mislead you about the more visceral frissions the film provides—it's as kinky, eccentric and bizarre as a film directed by the co-helmer of the spectacularly sleazy Mick Jagger shocker *Performance* should be. The late Cammell (who unfortunately blew his own head off in 1996) was a real deal lunatic who lived an extreme and extremely volatile life, only actually making a handful of pictures (including the blistering 1987 slasher deconstruction *White of the Eye*, another of my personal favorites)—but when he spoke, baby, he spoke loudly and, especially here, damned ferociously.

And though *Demon Seed* is set in a world of harsh edges, speculative science and malevolent robots, Cammell chooses to accentuate the more organic angles of the tale; this is after all an exploitation film about a computer fucking, or rather, raping, a woman in order to create a kind of bionic bastard. During the pivotal and perverse fornication sequence, Cammell spins the picture into hallucinogenic visual overdrive, blasting colorful wormholes and violent editing spasms across the screen in a miasma of melty eyeball-spinning bliss. Then, at *Demon Seed*'s halfway point as Susan begins her rapidly belly-swelling incubation period, various people stumble into the home only to be dispatched by the defensive Proteus. For these sequences, Cammell temporarily abandons his elegant sexual science approach and goes for outrageous horror-show guignol, as the nest-protecting computer miraculously transforms into a smooth, pulsing and homicidal, human-crushing Rubik's Cube, a writhing, larger than life riff on the decade-later Lament Configuration in Clive Barker's *Hellraiser*. It's out of leftfield elements like this that make *Demon Seed* such a head-spinning, brilliant and disorienting cinematic experience.

Firmly set in the center of *Demon Seed*'s weird celluloid universe, and indeed the source of much of the picture's dramatic power, is the low, controlled and chilling passive-aggressive vocal persona of Proteus himself, a tour de force turn by *The Man From U.N.C.L.E*'s Robert Vaughan. Forget Hal, Vaughan's Proteus is a sexually aware device that tries to imitate his human masters but just can't find the eye of the mortal needle.

There's a real vulnerability to the omnipresent Proteus that, whether vindictively punishing Susan by cranking the heat in the house to lethal levels or cooing like a microchip Casanova, makes him both a scary and realistic screen presence. If I ran the world, 1977 would have been the year Robert Vaughan took home the Oscar. But, alas, I don't and he didn't.

As decadent and out of control as *Demon Seed* may appear to be, Cammell knew exactly what he was doing, making a futuristic sex thriller by way of brain melting acid trip; a smart, frightening, sexy and one of a kind movie that also stands as the last great science fiction film of the decade. And George, if you're reading this…Kiss my wookie.

THE DEVIL'S NIGHTMARE 1971

Starring Erika Blanc, Jean Servais and Daniel Emilfork
Written by Jean Brismee and Claude Garnier
Directed by Jean Brismee

According to the Bible, if one habitually indulges in any combination of The Seven Deadly Sins, the ultimate punishment is an eternity broiling in the flaming bowels of Hell. According to director Jean Brismee's 1971 Belgian/Italian sexploitation horror gem *The Devil's Nightmare*, however, any serious dabbling in capital vice will conjure up a see-through-negligee-wearing Erika Blanc (*The Night Evelyn Came Out of the Grave*) to shake her satanic tail feather before turning you into a quivering, whimpering mess of a man.

Methinks the Brismee fate beats the Bible any day.

Long lapsed into the public domain and known under scads of alternative titles, *The Devil's Nightmare* is a fantastic treat for fans of European genre pics and, despite its easy availability, isn't readily recognized and revered. The film begins in a sepia-toned version of Berlin in the waning days of WWII as, amidst grainy, poorly matched stock footage of falling bombs, the Baroness Von Rhoneberg painfully squeezes out her firstborn child…and promptly dies for her troubles. Deeply depressed by this widower making turn of events, the good Baron's saddened state deepens when he discovers that the surviving child is not the son he had hoped to sire, but rather a daughter, an omen that he believes will bring upon him a centuries-old family curse. Fearing the worst, the Baron nips this potentially devastating problem in the bud by impaling the screaming infant on the end of a bayonet.

Flash forward 25 years. A bus full of generally repellent tourists breaks down on mountainside and, after a chance encounter with a sickly, skinny, black-clad shepherd (*City of Lost Children*'s Daniel Emilfork), they're directed to the Baron's imposing, decrepit castle. Once there, the motley crew—which includes the gluttonous driver, a philandering husband, a money-grubbing hussy, a grumpy old man, a jealous wife, a morally conflicted priest and, um, a couple of hot lesbians—encounter a doubtful guest that even Edward Gorey couldn't have imagined: the Amazonian, hotter-that-Hell succubus Lisa Muller (Blanc). Before the long night is done, each and every one of these sinners will be saddled with fates far worse than death.

The Devil's Nightmare is a delightfully kitschy, lurid and thoroughly entertaining vintage Italian Gothic romp that offers many grimy charms. Brismee's direction is leering and fluid, echoing the best of Mario Bava (incidentally, Blanc also starred in the maestro's masterwork *Kill, Baby Kill*) and Antonio Margheretti (think *The Virgin of Nuremberg*); the production design by French porn vet (and Jean Rollin regular) Jio Berk is cheap, simple and incredibly effective; the dynamite fuzz guitar score by the legendary Alessandro Alessandroni (who worked alongside Ennio Morricone in many an Italian Western including Sergio Leone's '*Dollars*' trilogy), with its trippy female vocals and evil harpsichord is sexy, sinister and totally badass; the pre-*Se7en* mortal sins-themed script by Brismee and Claude Garnier (Jess Franco's *The Midnight Party*) is clever and amusing and the semi-explicit lesbian sex scene is smoldering. I only mention this sweaty, Sapphic sequence because I first saw the film as a kid under the title *The Devil Walks At Midnight* and no such frolicking was to be found. UK label Redemption rectified this omission and finally catching up to the completely out of leftfield coupling was a naughty revelation indeed. I'm a completist, what can I say…

Ultimately though, the main draw of *The Devil's Nightmare*—and indeed the reason I adore it—is watching the astonishing

Erika Blanc at her most malevolent

Blanc strut herself across the screen. Whether coyly slinking around in cleavage-revealing, hip-hugging black silk or physically distorting her almost makeup-free face into a hideously ugly, pasty and lipless menace, Lady Blanc simply steals the show. Still going strong at 69, the ever lovely actress may put this particular picture low on her resume, but I've yet to see her—or *any* Eurohorror actress, for that matter—perform this brilliantly in any film of this kind. She's the secret sauce in a yummy little romp that every '70s trash movie lover needs to know about.

June 2008

How did music become your life?

In the village of Soriano, where I grew up, there were small shops called Barber & Taylor shops and they had a myriad of instruments hanging on the walls. In between clients—or when there were no clients at all—anyone could play the mandolin or guitar or cello or clarinet...and that is how I started this journey. I am self-taught with no professional training.

Many fans know you from your work with Ennio Morricone on all those incredible Sergio Leone Westerns, especially your trademark whistle. When did you discover your talent for whistling?

Well, it was quite by accident that this became my trademark. During a recording session of music for an early film I was involved with, [composer] Nino Rota asked if anyone in the orchestra could whistle—I was playing guitar then. No one came forward so I said that I could try but couldn't promise anything. But it worked and that is how the quality of my whistle was discovered. By the time Ennio and I worked together, I was an expert!

Can you tell me about your initial work with Morricone? How free were you to experiment?

My work with Ennio was always engaging and always creative. Often I would suggest alternative styles in the execution of his written music, bringing in guitar—the whistling—some more rock-influenced sounds

Do you ever feel that you haven't received enough credit for your work on those incredible Westerns?

Oh yes, absolutely. But, that's life, I suppose.

Can you describe those prolific days working in the golden era of Italian cinema in the 1960s and 1970s? It must have been a very exciting time.

In those years we had so many wonderful directors in this country—Fellini, Pasolini, Risi, Germi, Leoni—and so many wonderful films were being made. After the success of *A Fistful of Dollars* we Italian musicians were kept very busy because so many Westerns were being made as well as horror films and other pictures that could be exported

easily to America and around the world. Also, my choir *The Cantoni Moderni di Alessandroni* was very much in demand for films and recordings. Yes as you say, it was a very exciting and incredibly busy time and I'll admit that I miss it.

One of my favorite scores of yours was for Jean Brismee's 1971 horror film The Devil's Nightmare. *What are your memories of that picture?*

I remember that film vaguely. It wasn't too bad as I recall. But after some 40 years—and a lot of music in between—I don't remember very much about my score!

Who did those haunting female vocals for the film's opening theme?

Ah, that would have been my late wife, Giulia De Mutiis.

Your work in the same year's Lady Frankenstein *is also brilliant, fully exploiting that distinctive fuzz guitar. What did you think of that film and of its American director, Mel Welles?*

That film is actually pretty good! One of my better horror scores, I think. I don't recall working with Mel Welles, however. As was often the case, he may have left it up to me to create the sound as I chose appropriate without too much interference on his part.

You've also worked with notorious Italian exploitation filmmaker Bruno Mattei on 1977's SS Extermination Camp. *What was Mattei like?*

Now that one was no great masterpiece, I can tell you that. In fact, I must admit that it was a very mediocre picture and I refer to both the film and the music itself. But I worked very well with Mattei and I found him to be a very nice man.

You worked on two adult films in 1980 with the great Joe D'Amato (Aristide Massachessi)...

Yes I did and you know, D'Amato was really amusing, a very colorful character. As far as my music on those pornographic pictures, the big difference was that, well I was obliged to think erotically, not horrifically. I think my work on those movies is pretty good and a lot of fun.

Your last credited film is 1998's Trinity Goes West. *Any plans to return to film composing?*

I would willingly compose more film scores but in Italy these days everything is motivated by politics for political ends. That is not for me. I am a free man and I would want my music free of obligations or constraints. Anyhow, I am glad that publishers are reprinting a lot of my music and that people are now buying the CD collections.

Your scores for horror films were so eccentric and interesting. Do you watch horror? Have you heard any music in horror that you really liked?

No, I have never watched or listened to horror except to compose for those horror movies I wrote the scores for. I simply followed my instincts. The bottom line is that I LOVE to create new sounds all the time and horror movies gave me great freedom to do that.

The unsung gentleman of Italian composers himself

IN THE FOLDS OF THE FLESH
1970

Starring Elanora Rossi-Drago, Pier Angeli and Fernando Sancho
Written and Directed by Sergio Bergonzelli

There really is something special about those saucy European sleaze horror films from the 1970s.

You know.

That unique blend of morally bankrupt, American-potboiler pulp-noir attitude combined with a distinct *haute couture*-informed Euro-sexuality and sensationally stylized level of graphic, phantasmagorical violence. Sigh. It just speaks to me, I guess. I worship Dario Argento, swoon over Sergio Martino, bite my lip at the name Leon Klimovsky, click my heels over the body of Antonio Bido, pump my fists at the mere mention of Lucio Fulci…yes, I love these men and the maniacal works of misbehaving, lush, junk-shock cinema they once slung (and in some cases, continue to admirably sling).

I've seen and owned so many fantastic Italian, Spanish and French genre films from this period that I consider myself something of a connoisseur, a man who knows and loves his Eurotrash and can differentiate between a really good lurid treat, a middling one and one that couldn't cut the mustard in an Erika Blanc/Edwidge Fenech sandwich (and good god is that not a smoking hot image?) And seeing as I also adore all kinds of weird art that carelessly careens wildly off the rails, it's my pleasure to prattle on here, in this particular chink of my *Blood Spattered Book* about a grimy little gem from Italo-trash veteran Sergio Bergonzelli (*Blood Delirium*), a picture that takes such pleasure in misbehaving on so many levels that it was literally—for me, anyway—love at first, long, livid look.

I'm talking about the obscure and gloriously nasty 1970 number *Nelle Pieghe Della Carne* (or *Les Endemoniadas* in Spain), known to a select few of its devout followers as *In the Folds of the Flesh*. This quasi-psychedelic, taboo teasing, overheated, dirty minded melodrama positions itself as a semi-serious study in Freudian theory

gone mad, but in reality the film is really an excuse to throw as much trippy, LSD-laced psycho-sexual insanity at the screen as humanly possible. And boy-oh-boy baby, it works.

Now, please be patient while I attempt to relate the unrepentantly insane plot:

Elanora Rossi Drago (Massimo Dallamano's kitschy version of *Dorian Gray*) stars as the prim but comely Lucille, the former housekeeper and now head of a twisted family that whiles away their days and nights in a crumbling coastal castle. 13 years prior, Lucille had been privy to the charming sight of her young charge Falesse (the late, lovely Pier Angeli who plays the dual role of Falesse and [SPOILER] Esther, and is at least 15 years too old for the part) being raped by her own father. When pop had popped, the humiliated and emotionally shattered Falesse effectively hacked off his horny, incestuous noggin with a razor-sharp saber.

An ex-convict (played by a gloriously greasy Fernando Sancho, the despicable mayor from *Return of the Blind Dead*) shows up one afternoon to confront Lucille, her foppish teenage son and the now completely stark-raving-mad Falesse about the crime, claiming he witnessed the impromptu midnight burial that followed, and is now demanding cash and rough sex to keep quiet. Lucille and Falesse reluctantly oblige the greedy, groping pig before Lucille administers a dose of lethal, choking cyanide to his bubble bath. The trio then hack him up and feed the less putrid parts to their flesh-eating pet buzzard.

Still with me? Good…

During all these dirty, sexual and violent escapades, Falesse keeps having color-soaked flashbacks of her old man getting jiggy and the post-coital decapitation that followed. Eventually more men come to the castle to (booty) call and they too become headless buzzard snacks. And in between all this hallucinogenic poking

Elanora Rossi-Drago and Pier Angeli in a literally wigged-out moment

and prodding, Falesse puts on reel-to-reel audio tapes of head-spinning sex talk and makes out with Lucille's son. We also learn that Lucille's fixation with cyanide stems from her youth in a Nazi concentration camp where she was spared from the gas showers that killed her mother in front of her because a gaggle of jackbooted Third Reich goons opted to gang rape her.

Then things get really weird when the supposedly dead and *sans tete* daughter-raping master of the house returns, unrecognizable to Lucille, claiming he was in hiding and had had a facelift. A Pandora's box of secrets and lies spills open and an already bonkers narrative vir- tually implodes in a soapy, bloody hyperbolic pipe bomb of silliness and über scuzz.

In the Folds of the Flesh has often been labeled a giallo picture, but I wouldn't call it one. There's no red velvet, prowling cameras or black leather-wearing masked killers about and the mystery itself leans more toward Harlequin than Hitchcock. What we have here instead is a film that tries so hard to be disturbing that it becomes almost endearing. And while a lot of the great Eurotrash thrillers of the period I so adore trade heavily on being as visceral and mean-spirited as possible, there's a bouncy

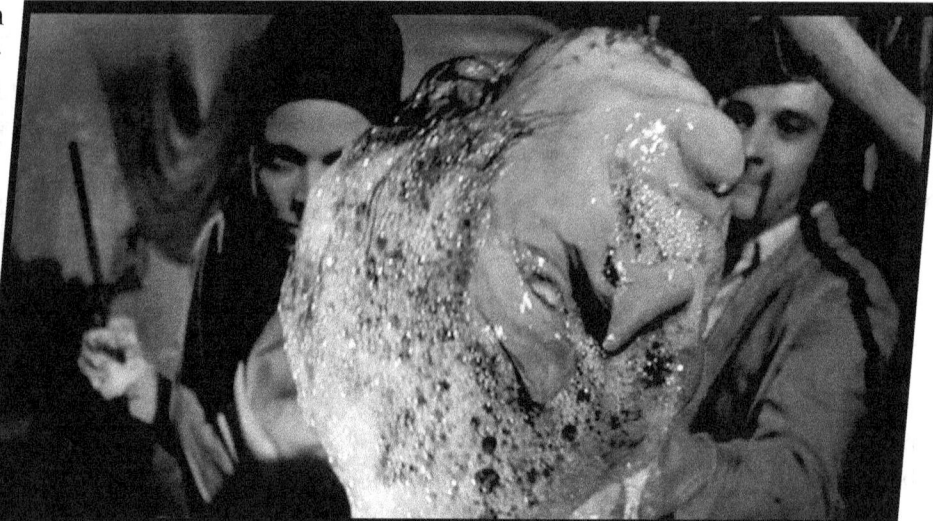

The old soapy head on a stick gag

B-movie sensibility at work here that keeps it all rather frothy and certainly the serpentine, ADD-afflicted plotline only jacks up the naughty fun. And surprisingly, the plentiful sex is never particularly graphic or gratuitous.

If, as many film historians cite, the first few years of every decade belong to the last, then *In the Folds of the Flesh* (the title is actually a nod to a Freud quote about memories lodged in the brain and not about the sweaty creases in the skin) is as much a product of the drug-drenched 1960s as it is of the sexually permissive 1970s. Bergonzelli's visual palette is all melting saturated colors, off kilter camera angles and choppy, schizoid editing, suggesting a Timothy Leary-lensed version of *Suspiria*.

I absolutely adore this perverse little flick and now, thanks to niche DVD imprint Severin Films, it ain't as hard to locate as it once was. If you have a taste for joyously twisted, brilliantly bad (ass) vintage exploitation, then this utterly mad Italian/Spanish sickie is for YOU…

A wild-eyed Pier Angeli

THE KEEP
1983

Starring Ian McKellen, Scott Glenn, Jurgen Prochnow and Gabriel Byrne
Based on the novel by F. Paul Wilson
Written and Directed by Michael Mann

When it comes to dark fantasy and horror filmmaking, I am and always will be a strong advocate for antirealism, which is to say I prefer my terrors to exist in a dream state, free of the pretentious shackles of narrative logic, existing in a world that is but a hazy impression of the mundane one in which we live.

This is why I hold the weird work of David Lynch, the fever dreams of Mario Bava and the late period surrealist shocks of Lucio Fulci in such reverent regard. Hell, I even adore Christophe Gans' big-screen adaptation of *Silent Hill* and laud it for, if nothing else, tapping into that nightmare logic where nothing makes sense, nothing is absolute and anything can—and usually does—happen.

This is also why I've always been a strong champion of Michael Mann's evocative, absurd, flawed and occasionally transcendent 1983 cinematic adaptation of author F. Paul Wilson's terrifying novel *The Keep*, a movie that was cut upon its release by a nervous studio, ignored by audiences, deplored by critics, rejected by its source scribe and generally forgotten. Though the ensuing years have seen it accumulate a quiet cult following, the movie is still as of this writing unavailable on DVD. But as usual, I get ahead of myself.

Allow me to muse…

In the darkest days of WWII, a wayward band of SS troops, led by the sympathetic Captain Woermann (Jurgen Prochnow of *Das Boot* and Uwe Boll's *House of the Dead* fame) find themselves snaking around Romania, specifically a remote, fog-drenched village in the midst of a mountain pass. On the outskirts of this village sits a monolithic fortress, a Keep, a shrine of sorts that the locals insist houses an ancient evil, and where the Nazis choose to set up their stronghold.

Against the conflicted Woermann's wishes, the greedy Third Reich droogs begin secretly prying off the protective silver crosses that line the walls and, in an especially eerie sequence, unleash a pulsing, chasm-dwelling, sentient white light that promptly separates one unlucky stormtrooper's noggin from his neck. As even more of the men begin to meet their strange, untimely demises, grim reinforcements in the form of the ultra sadistic Major Kaempffer (a chilling Gabriel Byrne) and his troops roll into town, casually laying waste to the innocent villagers and enlisting an old, wheelchair-bound Jewish professor named Dr. Theodore Cuza (the great Ian McKellen) to aid them in deciphering the cryptic, possibly Hebrew scrawl on the walls left after each kill.

As Cuza soon discovers, the Nazi scum have indeed unleashed absolute evil in the form of a slowly evolving, muscle-necked demon named Molasar (Michael Carter), a force of darkness that was imprisoned inside the Keep centuries prior and with apparently very good reason. As the body count increases and a wave of madness and corruption oozes over the previously peaceful village, across the ocean a loner named Glaeken (Scott Glenn) is also drawn to the Keep, armed with a glowing staff, a chip the size of Gibraltar on his immortal shoulder, and

51

Scott Glen and Alberta Watson feel the power of *The Keep*.

The Keep is a film of many sensory pleasures and the key to truly enjoying it is to overlook its flaws.

a blind, instinctual drive to put the horrific Molasar back into his stony grave once and for all.

When *The Keep* was released in 1983, Mann was already a filmmaker of some note, having both written and directed the slicker-than-slick 1981 James Caan thriller *Thief* (he was still a year shy of the brilliant *Miami Vice*, an amazing, ahead-of-its-time TV show that I STILL swear by) and Wilson's skin-crawling best seller had already found its way to paperback. Almost immediately it became clear that fans of that book were up in arms at Mann's big screen stab at the story. Chief among their many gripes was the fact that Molasar had been inexplicably altered from a bloodsucking ageless vampire into a hulking skull-faced prosthetic brute with laser beam eyes. Wilson himself was aghast, not only by the picture's many changes, but also because of its disjointed tone and improper pacing; the author went as far as to publicly denounce *The Keep* as an "incomprehensible mess."

Why the vampirism angle was excised is anybody's guess; perhaps it was due to the fact that in the early '80s Hollywood vampirism had, as it does every so often, burned out its popularity coil. The only other vampire film of 1983, *The Hunger,* also betrayed its source novel (by Whitley Strieber) by keeping its fangs similarly in check, emphasizing slick visuals and art-directed sex over traditional undead thrills. It's very possible that the good folks at Paramount gingerly persuaded Mann to give the blood sucking a break and tailor the tale to the glossier, less earthy, increasingly synthetic MTV-driven decade. As for the admittedly jarring jumps in logic and plot, rumor has it that Mann's final cut of the film was almost three hours long and the studio simply opted to shave it down to smithereens for cynical, practical exhibition purposes.

But again, I digress.

Let's get down to the meat of this dark entry, the reason I'm risking developing carpal tunnel syndrome writing about this too often maligned motion picture. Well, put simply, I fucking love *The Keep* and I don't care who knows it. I'm painfully aware of the source novel deviations; I loved the book too. But what some people fail to grasp is that what works on page doesn't necessarily work onscreen—one being a literary medium, the other being primarily visual and sensory—and perhaps the changes were warranted. Not only that, but the passage of time has proven Michael Mann to be an auteur, a stylist with a creative palette completely unique to him and no one else. Looking back on *The Keep* today, we can see a young filmmaker experimenting, finding and perfecting his visual and tonal vocabulary simply using the Wilson novel as a framing device. Blue lights streaming though broken windows, slow pans across fog-soaked landscapes, outlandish, borderline ridiculous and otherworldly character behaviors and a sense of thick, oppressive and unwavering tension—they're all here in their early '80s glory. Who gives a damn if they aren't in the novel? The novel has its own charms. But one thing the novel does NOT have is a score by motherfucking Tangerine Dream…

Yes. Let's address that. Tangerine Dream. A collective of German experimental electronic musicians led by composer Christopher Franke, the noted band had previously laid down hypnotic cinematic soundscapes for William Friedkin's *Sorcerer*, Michael Laughlin's *Strange Behavior*, Mann's own aforementioned film noir *Thief,* and would later sculpt deft music for Ridley Scott's *Legend* and Kathryn Bigelow's *Near Dark*. Their efforts on *The Keep* are like aural glue, an endless wave of thick analog synth music that, even when inappropriate (as in that scene where the soldiers chisel the beautifully detailed silver cross off the keep's wall), gel the film together, becoming as vital to the identity of the movie as the sets, the suffocating mists, the top notch cast and the goofy looking yet imposing and ultimately effective Molasar himself.

In fact, if you're a fan of the works of German art house director Werner Herzog (which I most certainly am), you'll see incredible, perhaps intentional, perhaps not, parallels between Mann's work with Tangerine Dream and Herzog's collaborations with composer Florian Fricke, aka Popul Vuh. The slow, meditative sequence where Glaeken's ship crosses the ocean is eerily akin the scene where Dracula's ghost ship drifts the high seas in Herzog's 1979 remake of *Nosferatu* and the opening images of the fog-shrouded, mountain-sealed Romanian village look and sound like they were pulled wholesale out of Herzog's breathtaking 1972 historical psychodrama *Aguirre: The Wrath of God*.

However you see *The Keep* (and again, as of this writing, VHS and laserdisc are your only options), the bottom line is to just see it. It is a film of many sensory pleasures and the key to truly enjoying it is to overlook its flaws, its lapses in logic, its often dated visual effects and let it simply wash over you, to sink into it and perceive it like an opium-inflicted hallucination. If nothing else, *The Keep* most certainly makes a case for the horror film as an outlet for subconscious art, as a surreal dark dream, as an experience that you react to not intellectually, but physically and emotionally.

LAIR OF THE WHITE WORM 1988

Starring Sammi Davis, Amanda Donohoe, Catherine Oxenberg and Hugh Grant
Based on the story by Bram Stoker
Written and Directed by Ken Russell

Ken Russell is insane. I say this with some authority, as I've seen pretty much every film the eccentric Brit has helmed since 1967's goofy spy send-up *Billion Dollar Brain*, right through to his completely daft blood-sucking boobies entry in the upcoming hot-and-cold horror omnibus *Trapped Ashes*. I've even read his autobiography, twice. His landmark 1971 cinematic freak-out *The Devils* still stands as one of my top-5 favorite filmed meditations on sin, lust and religious corruption. And though Russell has garnered his greatest accolades with both that brilliant pic and his hyperkinetic 1975 adaptation of The Who's rock opera *Tommy*, I think my single favorite Ken Russell joint is a steamy little number that not many horror

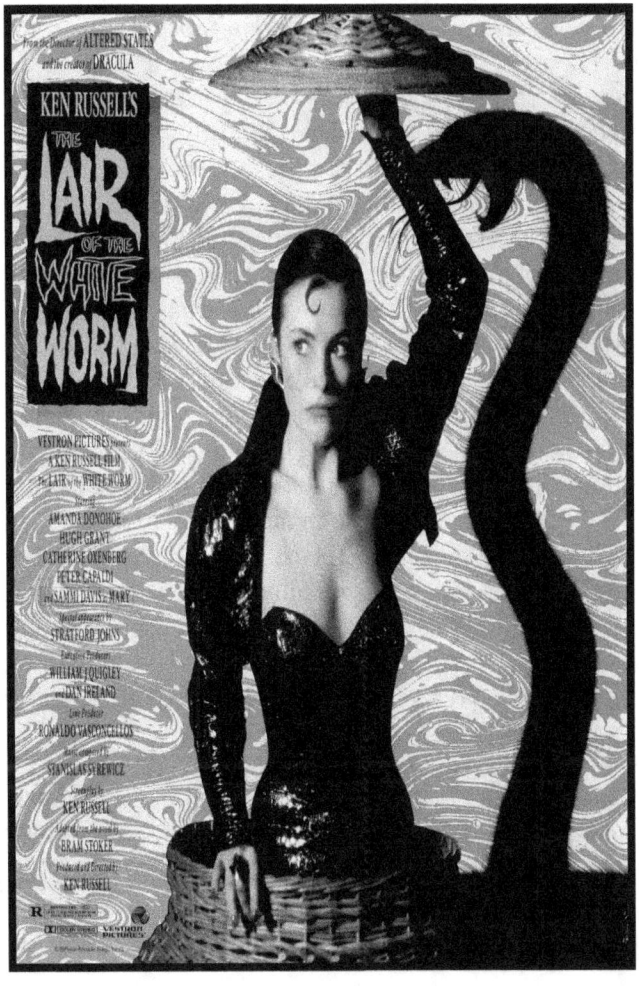

This German lobby card features one the many unhinged dream sequences in *Lair of the White Worm*.

fans know about but a handful of us faithfully still rave over. I speak now about the 93-minute stretch of coiled, semi-offensive, quintessentially Ken Russell descent into funny, freeform perversion, the dirty-minded 1988 blackly comic shocker *The Lair of the White Worm*.

Loosely (and brother, I mean loosely) based on the considerably less saucy short story by mad Irishman (and of course, *Dracula* mastermind) Bram Stoker, *The Lair of the White Worm* was part of a package deal of movies the wacky filmmaker produced and directed for the fledgling (now defunct) theatrical wing of Vestron Pictures, a lower budget but high concept multi-genre freak out that defied easy classification. The movie tells the tail-eating tale of orphaned sisters Mary (the delightful Sammi Davis) and Eve (Catherine Oxenberg), two lasses who while away their days happily running their parent's quaint country guesthouse and fritter away their nights flirting with bratty local Lord James Dampton (a charming, early turn by future megastar Hugh Grant) and visiting Scottish archaeologist Angus Flint (Peter Capaldi). When hapless, kilt-clad Indiana Jones clone Flint unearths an unclassifiable, monstrous reptile skull in a buried pagan convent near the girl's property, a midnight visit is paid by their mysterious, reclusive and undeniably gorgeous neighbor Lady Sylvia Marsh (Amanda Donohoe).

Seems the slinky Marsh isn't only an ultra rich, man-hungry mama but a deadly, venom-spitting, snake-worshipping vampire hellcat too. She's a high priestess of the cult of Dionin, a giant flesh-eating serpent whose legions have plagued the village since Christ was a carpenter. After the cooing Marsh steals the ancient serpent noggin, she soon learns that the beautiful Eve hasn't yet had her own treasures plundered, and the depraved aristocrat devises a plot to serve her current, very-much-alive and starving, scaly, cave-dwelling master a menu of virgin à la carte. In the meantime, Marsh makes do with vomiting poison on a cross, provokes mind-blowing, theologically offensive hallucinations in the sweet, cheerful Mary (including a devastating mass murder/sexual assault of a legion of nuns that echoes *The Devils* rape of Christ), vampirizes a chubby beat cop and gives a halitosis-plagued boy scout the worst blowjob of his short, horny life.

There are so many dirty delights to savor in *The Lair of the White Worm*. It's a virtual pig-out of cheerfully rude, typically bad Ken Russell behavior. But outside of the plethora of hallucinatory, eye-smacking imagery, an oddball cast of characters and general yummy nastiness that smothers virtually every frame, it's the presence of the lithe, sexually sophisticated Donohoe herself that truly hits this epic of raunchy shock out of the park. Whether brashly parading about town in knee-kissing kinky boots, or baring her elongated, crotch-positioned, venom-tipped canines, or licking her damp lips seductively before inserting a massive phallus into her various victims' naughty bits, Donohoe is nothing short of ribald royalty. She's the quintessential campy Russell anti-heroine, all taboo sex and hypnotic, winking menace, the logical, blood-hungry, supernatural successor to Kathleen Turner's deeply troubled, animalistic dominatrix in Russell's overheated X-rated 1985 melodrama *Crimes of Passion* (also distributed by Vestron).

The lanky, toned and happily uninhibited actress would also appear in one more Russell/Vestron vehicle, the same year's considerably better behaved but no less passionate D.H. Lawrence prequel *The Rainbow*, in addition to the previous years incredibly underrated melodrama *Castaway*, a film directed by another mad Brit auteur, Nicolas Roeg, and co-starring a drunk and shockingly hirsute Oliver Reed. Eventually she would settle into a high profile role in TV's *L.A. Law* but it is with this deliriously madcap, one of a kind venture into deepest, darkest irreverent Russelldom that Lady Donohoe's persona would be irrevocably etched into horror and cult film cinema history.

If you don't take the time to seek out *The Lair of the White Worm* and revel in its many hot, demented charms, may Dionin himself eat your balls for breakfast.

AN INTERVIEW WITH ACTRESS AMANDA DONOHOE

September 2008

The first time I saw you was in Nicolas Roeg's Castaway. *What are your memories of that haunting, dreamlike picture?*

Castaway was only the second movie I had made and my first leading role so I was still a complete novice and I was overwhelmed and delighted to be working with two of my heroes of cinema, Nic Roeg and, of course, Oliver Reed. I had no idea, however, how difficult it would be dealing with a leading man who, upon reflection, was well on his way to becoming a chronic alcoholic. The rest is history as they say.

Was it a difficult shoot, then?

Well, filming in the Seychelles could be grueling at times, but we always managed to have a lot of fun and Oliver was always extremely professional…it was the times in between filming that were rather more challenging. "One more day in fucking paradise," was the daily motto.

It's such an odd, beautiful and underrated film…

I haven't watched the movie for years, but yes I'd agree it is indeed strange and beautiful as was Lucy Irvine's book from which the screenplay was adapted.

How did you land on Ken Russell's radar for those two incredible Vestron pictures?

Ken Russell saw *Castaway* and, of course, he knew Nic Roeg very well. They were the *enfant terribles* of the British film industry at one time, after all. I think that's how it happened, anyway.

Was Ken as charmingly bizarre as his words and his work would lead us to believe?

Oh yes! Absolutely. Ken was one of the most delightfully strange artists I've worked with. And you know his body of work is still more interesting, provocative and challenging than 90% of the movies made in the last three decades. As are Roeg's in my humble opinion…

Did anyone on the set of Lair of the White Worm *actually read the original Stoker text?*

I'm not sure if they did or not but I know that I did not read the Stoker novel and well, let's face it, it was a Ken Russell film so it really didn't matter! (Laughs)

I'm absolutely in love with the film, but I don't know of many others who are as devoted to it as I am. Am I wrong?

Lady Sylvia (Amanda Donohoe) prepares a sacrifice for the White Worm.

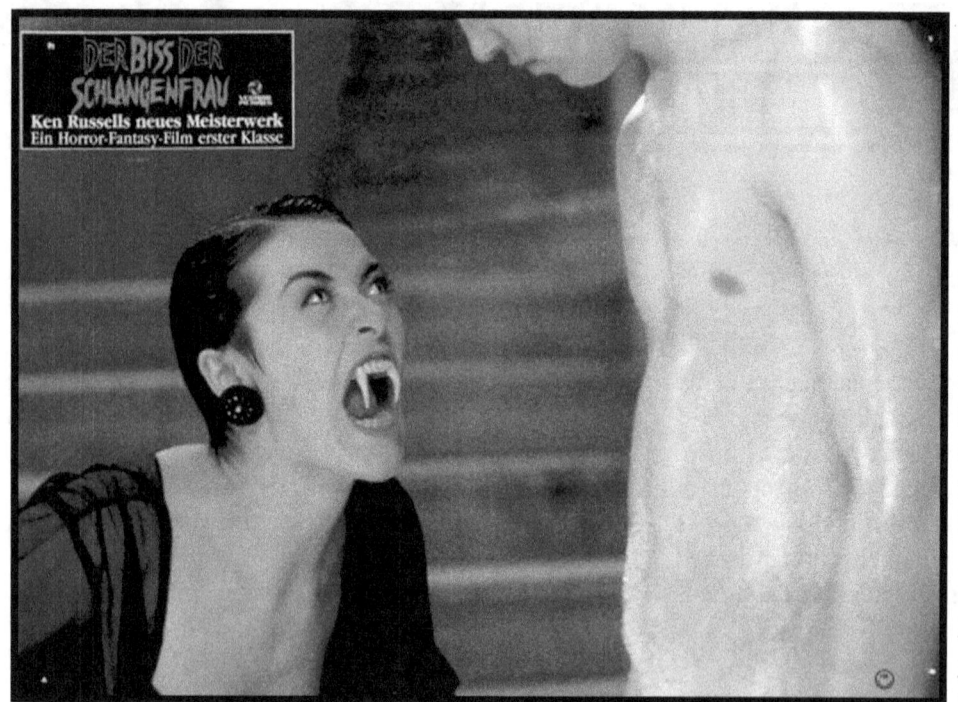

Well, I think it depends which kind of a movie fan you talk to. Apparently it's heavily downloaded on in the UK, as are clips of me as Lady Sylvia on YouTube.

Why wasn't there a sequel to Lair*? I remember hearing something about the possibility…*

There was talk, years ago, of a sequel, but I wanted to move on. And I think Hugh Grant was a little too busy with other things by then!

Your dedication to socialism and your sexuality have always been a strong part of your public identity. But have any of the edgier scenes you've done in these early works—like the gleefully perverse hallucinations in Lair*, the frequent nudity in* Castaway*, etc., ever put you in a position where you're called to defend your devout, equally well-publicized, feminist stance?*

It's true that I was breaking taboos in those days but it seems that nothing is shocking to the public anymore, least of all extreme violence as entertainment, which saddens me. I'm rather pleased though that sex and sexuality in general are so much more accepted and talked about.

As far as defending my work from a feminist point of view, feminism, in its purest sense, means, quite simply, that one supports the concept of the equality of the sexes; "An extended recognition of the claims [equal rights] of women" as defined by the *Oxford Concise Dictionary*. This has nothing to do with nudity in art, or cinema. It is a political point of view and a strong personal belief that is thankfully, now, enshrined by law.

From your early work with Adam Ant to Roeg to Russell—you seem to gravitate towards eccentric artists and they seem to bring out the best in you. Can you comment?

Yes, and I still gravitate toward eccentric artists in cinema as well as other creative fields. After all the glitz, glamour and artifice of living in Hollywood, I find them refreshingly direct and irreverent. In fact I live with one such artist now. His field of expertise is sound and some of his stuff is pretty radical which, of course, I love.

LAND OF THE MINOTAUR
1976

Starring Donald Pleasence, Peter Cushing,
Luan Peters and Nikos Verlekis
Written by Arthur Rowe
Directed by Kostas Karagiannis

Sometimes I feel that there are certain pictures out there that I and I alone am in love with, that are speaking exclusively to me. I say this because it seems like everyone else with a pulse is either oblivious to the following flick or has callously deemed it to be dung. The strange sliver of celluloid of which I so highly speak—and again, so effectively speaks to me—is Kostas Karagiannis' creepy 1976 shocker *The Devil's Men*, known to us schmucks on North American shores as *Land of the Minotaur*. Released in 1977 in the U.S. by exploitation house Crown International to a—not bad at all—theatrical and drive-in box office, the film has been pretty easy to find on home viewing formats, popping up in rough looking pan and scan VHS versions and dodgy DVD releases here and in equally ugly (but thankfully uncut) videos in the UK. And yet, again, I've yet to hear anyone else champion its virtues.

I do believe it's time to do so.

On the outskirts of a remote, inland village in beautiful, picturesque Greece (Aris Stavrou's photography is occasionally breathtaking), something secret, insidious, clandestine and palpably evil lurks, sucking every too-curious young tourist into its dark depths and swallowing them whole. As the ever-expanding list of the curious missing travelers increases, an eccentric local Priest (the great Donald Pleasence) begins to suspect that a cult of mountain-dwelling, black-hooded, Minotaur-worshipping Satanists have gained a stronghold, sacrificing every pretty young thing in their path to their titular stone hoof-and-horned, steam-belching deity.

A battle of theological wits ensues between the fraught Father and the ultra-wicked village Magistrate/covert cult leader Baron Corofax (the perhaps even greater Peter Cushing in rare, full-on chin-stroking villain mode) and by the time the smoke clears and the last drop of crudely spilled virgin blood dries, only one of these admirably dedicated and faithful men will be left standing.

A British/Greek co-production, *Land of the Minotaur* was indeed initially released in the UK under its original title *The Devil's Men* and, after cutting a few bits of blood and boob action to provide a PG rating, spat out Stateside under its more lurid moniker. Slapped with one of the more outrageous, colorful and almost completely misleading exploitation movie posters of the 1970s ("Half Man! Half Beast! Trapped in a Land Forgotten by Time!"), the picture was wedged onto the bottom half of a Crown double bill, pulling in the pundits, who were expecting an action-packed genre picture, before fading into B-movie oblivion and budget video waste bins everywhere.

But let's get back to the reasons I so blatantly kneel before its bull-headed altar.

skin.

Drenched in an arid atmosphere reminiscent of vintage Sergio Leone, *Land of the Minotaur* is a picture that demands an open mind and, perhaps more importantly, an open ear. See, part of the soul-shuddering secret of the film, outside of the effortlessly engaging lead turns from veteran British horror pros Cushing and Pleasence (working together here for the first time since 1960's masterful *The Flesh and the Fiends*, another of my personal favorites), is an absolutely first rate experimental low frequency electronic score by the iconic composer/pop guru Brian Eno. The former Roxy Music mastermind coats this admittedly molasses-paced flick with speaker-throbbing drones, eerie synthesizer washes and throbbing pulses that render the flick almost meditative. It's a case study for any serious horror movie-minded music maker on how to milk unease out of imagery and the fact that this score isn't available in any isolated form on CD or vinyl or anything is a very serious cinematic crime that will hopefully one day be rectified.

I really like *Land of the Minotaur*. Make no mistake, it's a trash exploitation film (it was after all written by junk TV scribe Arthur Rowe) but it's junk that's filtered through a very stylized, haunting, arthouse sensibility. Don't be swayed by the negative mainstream reviews and general horror film press silence. There's something special in this one…trust me. I can't be the only one who likes it. Can I?

I first saw *Land of the Minotaur* during one of my indiscriminate Friday night teenage video rental binges in the mid '80s, duped, just like that legion of kids in 1977, by that beautiful, busy cover graphic. And though I did not get the promised epic I had hoped for, what I did get was something far darker, stranger, solemn, moody and bizarre. Something that maybe wasn't a good movie per se, but a picture that had a suffocating ambience and somber charm that really wormed its way under my

THE LAST MAN ON EARTH 1964

Starring Vincent Price, Franca Bettoia,
Giacomo Rossi-Stuart
Based on the Novel by Richard Matheson
Written by Logan Swanson (Richard Matheson) and
Ubaldo Ragona
Directed by Ubaldo Ragona and Sidney Salkow

I do declare that the time is right for a deeper look at Sidney Salkow and Ubaldo Ragona's 1964 Vincent Price vehicle *The Last Man on Earth*, the first (and to date, best) stab at adapting Richard Matheson's still blistering existential 1954 vampire novella *I Am Legend*. Written, then disowned, by the notoriously cranky author, the low-budget Robert Lippert (*The Earth Dies Screaming*) Italian/U.S. co-production has consistently been dismissed as a failed attempt to capture the psyche-destroying, bloodsucker staking exploits of eternally put upon virus survivor Robert Neville. And yet, as an avid follower and passionate devotee of the source text since I was but a wee lad, I have very little idea why. Though it inexplicably changes its hero's name from Neville to Morgan, and tweaks the ending somewhat, it otherwise seldom strays from the novella's narrative and perfectly captures its bleaker-than-bleak tone and downbeat mood.

Dr. Robert Morgan (Price) is not a well man. A mysterious airborne, plague-bearing dust storm has smothered the world, killing every man, woman and child and reviving them as sluggish, dull-witted, eternally ravenous vampires. And yet, somehow, some way, Morgan has remained immune, completely unscathed…well, physically, anyway. He lives his life like a machine, by day rising early, clearing the streets of comatose, emaciated ghouls and throwing their barely living bodies into an eternally burning tar pit, tracking the sleeping stronger ones to their lairs and driving his specially made stakes through their hearts.

But by night, when the sun sinks below the horizon, the fanged echoes of mankind come a-crawling out of their hiding spots, stumbling towards Morgan's garlic-and-mirror-fortified bungalow, clawing at his windows, screaming for his flesh and his blood. Such nerve shredding conditions might drive a weaker man to madness— though he skirts insanity often, Morgan instead opts to play his jazz records loud, pour a scotch, crawl into bed, squish a pillow against his head and wait, always wait, for the break of day when he'll get up and start the horrible cycle all over again. Unbeknownst to Morgan however, he's being watched by something other than the monsters, something that views him as an even bigger threat than the red-eyed viral vampires themselves.

The history of *I Am Legend* and its checkered journey to screen is rather fascinating. Published in 1954 by the young author, Matheson's gripping, intelligent and horrifying novella became a hit in sci-fi/dark fantasy/pulp fiction circles, landing squarely on the radar of fledgling UK studio Hammer Films. The lads at Hammer commissioned Matheson to adapt his story for the screenplay, which he did, reportedly brilliantly and faithfully from a straightforward text that almost read like a script to begin with. But, when the British censor skimmed the script, they were disgusted, promising that the downbeat, violent and depressing film would never, ever get passed. Hammer, still in their infancy, were terrified of the all powerful, commercially necessary censor board and released Matheson from his contract, his screenplay left untouched and unfilmed.

The property floated around for years before American born, British-based B-movie producer Robert Lippert got his mitts on it, finally inking an Italian co-production deal, oddly altering the script, hiring a fresh-from-Cormanville Vincent Price to play the lead and shooting the whole affair on a shoestring in Rome. When Matheson heard of the changes and rewrites to his script, and the casting of the larger than life Price as his reluctant working class hero Robert Neville, he balked and demanded his name be removed from the credits, instead sticking his oft-used pseudonym Logan Swanson on the final print. The movie was dumped into drive-ins, sneered at by critics, slammed for its wrong-headed casting and almost completely forgotten.

But what makes *The Last Man on Earth* the superior cinematic vision of Matheson's somber, frightening text is the profound way it handles Morgan/Neville's search for grim purpose. His is a life pushed to the brink and beyond and yet, as his heroic, defiant nature dictates, he fights back; through his terrifying nights, his blood-drenched days and his bittersweet dawns, Morgan refuses to succumb to his hopeless situation, refuses to even abandon his ramshackle bungalow. He becomes a kind of lone wolf, a vigilante, then a kind of prophet and finally a martyr, but always he's a caretaker, one whose life's work is to dispose of the subhuman monsters that have insidiously infested what was once a bright and beautiful world and have so cruelly cannibalized any fond memories he may have once had of anything resembling a happy life. And though they come to scrape at his windows like clockwork and though the rotting females pout and slink in a vulgar attempt to arouse him, he accepts the vampires, he adapts. To quote Matheson from an interview I conducted with him four years ago, it's the ultimate "portrait of an everyday Joe confronted with the arcane and emerging somewhat triumphant."

Even more resonant is the fact that *The Last Man on Earth* retains the absolutely pivotal character of Ben Cortman (though Anthony Zerbe's mentally unbalanced mutant albino cult leader Mathias in *The Omega Man* is certainly a loose variation on him). If you've read the novel, you'll recall that Ben Cortman was a friend, neighbor and colleague to Robert Neville who, post plague, became his chief vampiric adversary. Along with his tireless pack of drooling undead, Cortman is really Neville's perverted connection to his former humanity, a distorted nightmare logic vision of the man he once was. Over the span of time that the action in Matheson's story unfolds, the presence of Ben Cortman is both horrific and hopeful, distilling our hero's misery and re-focusing it as anger, as a need, a divine mission to kill Cortman, a desire that almost single handedly saves him from suicide. Cortman is in essence Neville's "El Dorado," his quest, his reason for waking, yet the kind of quest in which the searcher secretly pines to never complete, lest he be left with nothing to chase. *Last Man* keeps this disturbing dichotomy and mutually corrosive relationship wholly intact. In flashback, the film shows Ben Cortman (here played by *Kill Baby Kill*'s Giacomo Rossi-Stuart) and Morgan socializing at their children's birthday parties, then trying to develop a cure for the plague, before finally emerging as otherworldly enemies, as a constantly reversing of the hunter/prey dynamic.

It's a crucial narrative element that's deftly handled and is both appropriately unsettling and almost overwhelmingly tragic.

Just as beautifully rendered are the final days in the lives of Morgan's wife and daughter. As the rapidly disintegrating government insists on incineration of the deceased plague victims remains, Morgan, in a temporary fit of unbearable grief and searing madness, goes after the federal body burners in a vain attempt to rescue his little girl's corpse from the fire. When he returns home, morally beaten and empty handed to find his wife dead, he takes her corpse to a nearby field for a proper burial. Later that night, while Morgan reclines in a chair and waits for the inevitable, á la *The Monkey's Paw*, his spouse's now gurgled voice chants, "Robert, Robert…" Her unseen dirty and bloodless hands twisting the door handle, as she grins and moves in to give her still-living husband the kiss of death. To bastardize a popular movie poster tagline, if this lyrical, nightmarish sequence doesn't make your skin crawl, then it must be too fucking tight.

And what of poor Vincent Price, the chief reason Richard Matheson turned up his nose at the film to begin with? How does this hammy, wonderfully theatrical icon of horror fare as the haunted, tortured last living man on the planet? In the context of the film, fucking great, I say. Price's hangdog face, his wounded visage and melancholy internal monologue voiceovers are amazing and, if not quite the blue-collar Neville of the book, his Robert Morgan is never anything but believable and sympathetic.

Ultimately however, the three (four if you count Romero's 1968 *Legend* rip-off *Night of the Living Dead*) filmed versions of Matheson's soul-destroying nihilist masterwork fail to translate his unpretentious majesty verbatim, but really, why would you want them too? Movies are dreams. They should be visions of their inspirations, not duplicating them, but rather riffing on them, like great pop music cover songs. I love *The Omega Man* for its bombast, its '70s action movie bravado, its then topical sexual/racial politics and of course, that brilliant Ron (*Doctor Who*) Grainer score. I dig the recent Will Smith version for its haunting urban decay tableaux and its isolation and magnification of the heart-sinking Neville/dog incident. But when it all comes down the pipe, the perhaps accidentally brilliant *The Last Man on Earth* is the only one thus far that has managed to exist as an aggressively depressing and lyrical poetic nightmare, taking all that was profound and painful in the source text and re-presenting it as a low budget but evocative and funereal slice of pulp intellectual B-movie bliss.

Flawed but unforgettable, *The Last Man on Earth* deserves multiple viewings and a secure place in the annals of classic horror cinema. Best of all, it's long lapsed into the public domain and can be found haunting dollar stores across the world for less than a buck, so for God's sake man/woman, what paltry excuse can you muster to NOT see it?

AN INTERVIEW WITH WRITER RICHARD MATHESON

August 2006

What were the chief objections that Hammer had with your original I Am Legend *screenplay?*

Anthony Hinds at Hammer told me that the British censor simply wouldn't pass it because it was too violent and dark, which I thought was absurd. I know that they had a lot of problems over their early *Dracula* films so the censor wouldn't let them get away with anything at that point. But it wasn't any specific reason.

I know you've been very vocal about your distaste for Vincent Price in the Neville/Morgan role in The Last Man on Earth. *Why is this exactly?*

I liked Vincent and he was a very good actor performing for the films I wrote for American-International. He was terribly miscast however. He was far too grand and mannered. He wasn't my Robert Neville.

Is there anything you like about the film?

Well, I've learned to appreciate it more than I did. But at the time I wasn't impressed at all, all those needless changes. This is why I signed off on the picture with my pseudonym, Logan Swanson.

In the opening credits for Boris Sagal's The Omega Man, *you are credited as the source for the story, but the title of* I Am Legend *itself is not mentioned…*

Well, that makes perfect sense, as *The Omega Man* has nothing to do with my novel at all. I didn't like that film one bit. I've never understood why Hollywood keeps adapting my book but changing it as well. It is an easily adaptable story and my original screenplay was perfectly fine. I seriously doubt I'll ever see a proper version made.

What are your thoughts on Romero's riff on your material, Night of the Living Dead?

I first saw his film on TV and wondered why someone made a version of my novel without telling me! It's a decent picture and George claims he didn't make any money on it. If he had, however, I would have felt much differently.

LEGEND OF THE WEREWOLF
1975

Starring Peter Cushing, Hugh Griffith, Ron Moody
and David Rintoul
Written by Anthony Hinds
Directed by Freddie Francis

The DVD and Blu-Ray revolution is a double-edged sword. The pro is that scads of previously unseen and/or impossible to locate international cult, horror and exploitation titles are now easily accessible to every Tom, Dick and Harry that cares to peek. The con is the same as the pro. See, when I was a lad, my insatiable hunger for darker strains of cinema was fueled by the fact that you just couldn't readily get access to the flicks that you read about in books. At the dawn of home video's long-running reign, a young film collector like myself had to dig deep, to search and burrow, follow dead alleys and cold trails, meet bootleggers on foggy piers and generally position themselves as an amateur Sherlock (or more appropriately, Sher*schlock*) Holmes. And when I did indeed find those titles that no one talked about, often they were so pricey that my already masturbation-strained, blistered hands had to be further irritated by all the damn driveway snow shoveling I'd have to do to afford them.

But I loved it. It was the quest, the thrill of the hunt that connected me even deeper to these flicks...I felt like I earned a sort of *right* to hold them, to watch them; there was a deep sense of pride and accomplishment when I placed them on my shelf.

So with essentially every single one of my heavy, spooled video treasures now available in some class of souped-up, cleaned-up, squeaky-clean, special edition, anamorphic, double disc, unrated DVD release, part of my ever-seeking horror heart has kinda croaked. Still, there are a few gems in my massive, moldy old VHS collection that have yet to properly worm their way onto the so-called superior digital mediums.

One of those rare birds is the unfortunately late, legendary, Oscar-winning British cinematographer (David Lynch's *The Elephant Man*) and horror filmmaker (*Dracula Has Risen From the Grave, Tales From the Crypt, Trog*) Freddie Francis' difficult-to-locate 1975 Hammeresque wolfman shocker *Legend of the Werewolf*.

Now, many of you know I live and work in Toronto, that I'm a Canadian, born and raised. For those of you who don't know this, please refer to the previous sentence. See, back in the day, there was a fledgling homegrown company at the foot of Spadina Ave. called Interglobal Home Video, a pretty wild budget imprint that would acquire all sorts of weird, obscure horror, sci-fi, melodrama and cult titles and spit them out in handsomely packaged, LP-speed VHS editions that were staples of my local K-Mart's wallet-soothing delete bins. Even though I had never heard of such pictures as *Sisters of Death, Nightmare in Wax* or *Persecution*, I happily nabbed them all. To my surprise, these low financial risk adventures in exploitation movie economics paid off and I was rewarded with a rich tapestry of violent, sexy, strange and colorful pictures that swam upstream from the more mainstream terrors I was accustomed to. In fact many of them jumped up on the riverbank and ran away. But out of the myriad of blindly bought oddball potboilers that still sit lining the walls of my creepy little basement office, *Legend of the Werewolf* remains one of the most elusive. And really, I have to ask why, because the movie, while certainly not a masterpiece, is anything but bad.

As noted horror hero Peter Cushing so helpfully explains in *Legend of the Werewolf*'s weird opening sequence, it has been said that the beasts of the forest shall watch over and protect human children on Christmas Eve, because, well, their forefathers and mothers did it for Jesus, so if they didn't do it too they'd be hypocrites. This bit of made up myth provides credibility for the ensuing tale of poor little Etoile, a baby, who after his immigrant parents are chomped on by a pack of starving wolves, is inexplicably adopted by the now-sated pack. He grows up like a sort of lupine Tarzan, a wild untamed thing who is eventually rescued by a sleazy carny (the amazing, wild-eyed actor Hugh Griffith from, among many, many other fine films, *Ben Hur*) and top billed in his skid row circus as the feral Wolf Boy. Eventually Etoile grows into a strapping young lad (played by the bland David Rintoul), who makes the rather startling discovery that, when under pressure of full moon, he grows fangs, sprouts fur, pops his shirt and ends up looking a lot like Oliver Reed did in Terence Fisher's 1961 Hammer horror classic *Curse of the Werewolf*. In fact Jimmy Evans' makeup schemes and the Christmas curse aren't the only things that recall that admittedly superior film. See, Etoile ends up ditching his promising career as a rabid roustabout and flees to turn late 19th-century Paris (the Fisher film was based on Guy Endore's novel *The Werewolf of Paris* and both pics were penned by Anthony Hinds, under his pseudonym John Elder) where he gets a gig working at a zoo run by *Oliver!* heavy Ron Moody and falls in love with a beautiful whore, a woman who—like Reed's squeeze in *Curse*—seems to temper his inner lycanthrope. Of course, all goes sour when a jealous Etoile turns wolfy and rips the throats out of the local bordello's patrons and it again falls on the narrow shoulders of Peter Cushing, here playing an intrepid police pathologist, to line Etoile's homicidal cloud with sweet silver.

Legend of the Werewolf was produced by Tyburn Films, a tiny UK studio founded by Francis' son Kevin and one that sought to capitalize on Hammer's massive, decade-spanning, international success. Problem was, by 1974 Hammer horror was already passé and, after one more picture (1975's fine John Hurt vehicle *The Ghoul*), Tyburn took a permanent dive. How a little outfit like Interglobal ended up distributing *Legend* is anyone's guess, but I'm certainly glad they did. Though hampered by its low budget, and plot familiarity—and acres removed from director Francis' best work (though it's about a gazillion times better than his worst film, 1970's caveman vs. Crawford opus *Trog*)—*Legend* is an incredibly well-paced, blackly humorous, creepy and very British slice of B-level brilliance that I hold close to my heart. This beaten up tape of mine has seen the insides of no

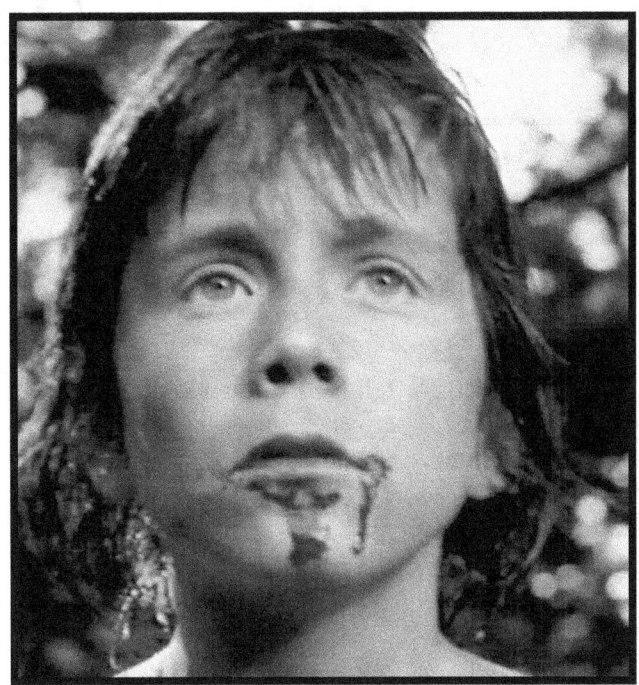

Little Etoile (Mark Weavers) tastes first blood.

less than seven VCRs and it still goes strong, it still pulls its LP-recorded weight with blood-dripping, hairy-backed finesse and flesh-shredding, electromagnetic grace.

And ultimately, *Legend of the Werewolf* means more to me because I know how bloody difficult it is to find, how even the darkest corners of eBay rarely offer a glimpse of its charms. It's part of my history, a sort of horrific Holy Grail, the symbolic piece of my "horror movie as life defining reason to pump blood and endure" philosophy.

It's why I do what I do.

The all grown up lycan (David Rintoul) in full blown wolf mode.

LIFEFORCE
1985

Starring Steve Railsback, Peter Firth,
Frank Finlay and Mathilda May
Written by Dan O'Bannon and Don Jakoby
Based on the Novel by Colin Wilson
Directed by Tobe Hooper

Don't attempt to tell me that director Tobe Hooper was responsible for only one massive dark fantasy classic in his admittedly up and down 30-plus years behind the lens. Because as important and untouchable his 1974 exercise in Texas chainsaw-wielding cannibal insanity is, I think it's his unclassifiable and ambitious 1985 sci-fi/horror epic *Lifeforce* that stands as his one *true* masterpiece.

Released the same year as cult favorites *Re-Animator*, *The Return of the Living Dead* (which Hooper was originally set to direct, in 3D no less), *Day of the Dead* and *Fright Night*, the filmmaker's mammoth, magnum space opera has rarely gotten its due and has never commanded the kind of fan base that those deservedly praised films command. But conceptually, *Lifeforce* is better than all of them combined and stands as a towering document of an ever-so-slightly bent artist at the peak of his unquestionably creative powers.

After the success of his Steven Spielberg- produced (and, if you believe the rumor mill, co-directed) 1982 horror hit *Poltergeist*, offers began flying fast and furious for Hooper. Eventually, the stogie-chomping Texan hung his Stetson on the hooks of fledgling Cannon Pictures, the company owned and operated by Golan/Globus—those oddball Israeli boys behind endless Ninja numbers, Chuck Bronson vigilante dramas and Chuck Norris shoot 'em ups—and secured an impressive, unprecedented three picture deal. Those films included the much maligned, woefully undervalued splattery spoof sequel to *The Texas Chain Saw Massacre* (which, incidentally, I also worship), a remake of the 1950s commies-on-the-loose creeper *Invaders from Mars* (which I initially disliked but has aged really well) and a big-budget adaptation of the 1976 Colin Wilson fantasy novel *The Space Vampires*.

The Cannon lads hired *Alien* vet (and eventual *Return of the Living Dead* director) Dan O'Bannon to pen the screenplay, which would soon be re-titled *Lifeforce*. The expensive movie was shot mostly in England and utilized an impressive array of classically trained British character actors (including *Star Trek: The Next Generation*'s Patrick Stewart in a really weird role I'm sure he'd love to forget), giving it an impressively sophisticated and linguistically cultured sheen.

The resulting picture, however, was anything but an immediate success, sharply dividing critics and fantasy film fans alike, with some citing it as one of the year's best while others declared it the bomb of the century.

You know where I stand.

Lifeforce details the dark drama surrounding the UK space shuttle *Churchill* as it crosses paths with an eerie derelict vessel that appears to resemble a giant bat. Inside the ghost ship, the crew discovers oceans of floating, desiccated creatures and a troika of super hot, nude alien humanoids encased in glass, which they

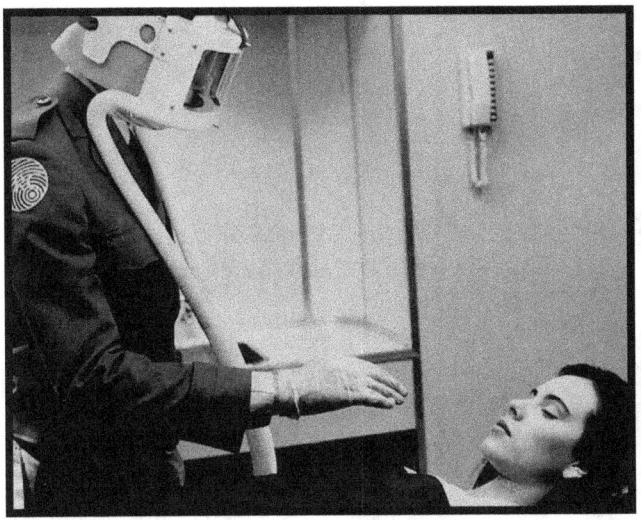

erroneously opt to bring on board. The beautiful ET's turn out to be energy-sucking vampires and their curvy leader (the impossibly stunning French actress/musician Mathilda May) proceeds to lay waste to *The Churchill*'s crew, draining them dry, save for one lovesick sap, a Col. Tom Carlson (*Helter Skelter*'s Steve Railsback).

The sexy galactic ghouls then make their way to earth and proceed to annihilate London, drinking energy and turning their infected victims into blood-hungry zombies. At the center of it all, the terminally confused Col. Colin Caine (Peter Firth) and Carlson (who shares an erotic, psychic link to May) race around trying to stop the escalating, apocalyptic madness.

The chief reason why many love *Lifeforce* is the same reason that others loathe it: the film is absolutely, inarguably, certifiably insane. It begins as an *Alien* clone, turns into a vampire flick, nods a few times to the Hammer film *Quatermass and the Pit* before morphing into a living dead drama, then a plague picture and then it settles on being an end of the world epic. All the while, the film refuses to acknowledge the hysterical silliness of its hyperactive, totally nuts narrative, choosing to play itself out instead as a deadly serious piece of glossy, grim pulp fiction.

Even if you don't fall squarely under *Lifeforce*'s unique spell, there's no denying that John (*Star Wars*) Dykstra's visual effects are still phenomenal and Nick Maley's dehydrated zombie puppets are elaborately terrifying. And the performances are fascinating and wildly eccentric. They range from flat-out fantastic (*The Pianist*'s Frank Finlay is commanding), to frenetic (Railsback is wild eyed from frame one), to unforgettable (May is femininity personified). The fact that more often than not, none of these actors seem to be coexisting in the same universe only adds to the delirious fun.

Hardcore *Lifeforce* fans have long been savvy to the fact that there are two radically different versions of the film in circulation. There's the original Cannon/Hooper 116-minute cut featuring a rollicking orchestral score by Henry Mancini and the 102-minute version prepared for American distributor Tri-Star. The Tri-Star version was the one widely distributed on VHS by now defunct label Vestron in the 1980s and I think it's the better of the two. The tighter running time perks up the pacing; the completely inappropriate opening voice over by *Chainsaw* narrator John Larroquette is removed, as is some laughable last reel dialogue between Firth and one of the male vamps; there's more zombies-in-London action and most importantly the score is considerably different.

While Mancini's lavish suites and cues are certainly majestic, the Tri-Star version replaces a lot of his material with an incredibly eerie, ambient strings and synth noise soundscape by the late composer Michael Kamen that adds deeply to the picture's creep factor. The version currently widely available on DVD from MGM is the original edit making the Vestron tape something of a collectible but no matter how you see this incredible motion picture; the bottom line is to simply see it. It's a breathtaking entertainment, trust me.

AN INTERVIEW WITH DIRECTOR TOBE HOOPER

August 2008

I've always been curious how you, a Texan tried and true, ended up working for that eccentric Israeli duo Golan and Globus on those three incredible Cannon pictures...

The bottom line was really simple: it was one of the first really big paying jobs offered to any director for a packaged deal, ever. It just didn't make any sense *not* to do it, really. And also, Menachem (Golan) and Yoram (Globus) just loved movies...absolutely loved them, so it was a pleasure.

Have you seen that crazy rock musical Golan directed, The Apple?

Oh, yeah! Yeah! That thing!

Not a good movie at all, but man, you're right...there's a real love of cinema there...

Yeah, a *total* love of cinema. He was also a real showman, maybe one of the last great ones. Now, things were really

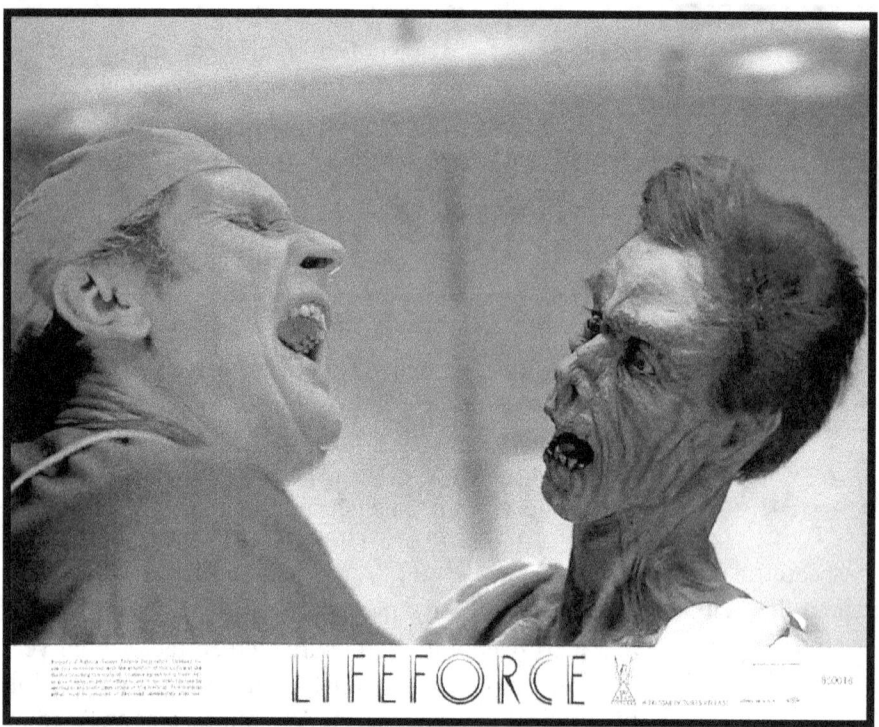

Lifeforce's vampires take much, much more than blood from their victims.

is—*critics and audiences either love it or hate it. I've yet to see a middle ground…*

Yeah, I haven't either…

Right. So what are your thoughts on the reception Lifeforce *received?*

Well, I mean at that point, everyone was really developing the idea that the value of a movie is based on the opening weekend's gross. You know, that whole summer blockbuster phenomenon? Well, it had already started. Anyway, I went to first screening and was terrified by the reaction so I went back to trim it and then it came out and well, the response wasn't fantastic. Probably if we had just called it *Space Vampires*, stuck with Colin Wilson's title, it would have placed it in the corporate at Cannon by the time I got there but you know, I could go in their office and in 90 seconds get a green light to do a movie based on a pitch. No intermediate development of script or anything. They'd ask me, "Tobe, when can we have this onscreen?" and I must say that I really liked that…

A bit reckless, perhaps...

Oh yes, certainly, they were more than a little bit reckless…

So your first picture for Cannon was Lifeforce. *Did that film have a bigger budget than* Poltergeist?

Yes, it was like 25 million, which was a lot for back then…

Col. Caine (Peter Firth) prepares for battle with the space vampires.

Was that intimidating at all, with that kind of money at stake?

Not at all. It was totally awesome. It was a step up. We had London rebuilt on the back lot with all the tubing for the flames and a hell of a lot of extras. It was magnificent. *Now, I've always been aware at how divisive* Lifeforce proper context to appreciate it.

Were you stung by some of the negative reviews?

A little bit, yes. But afterwards, I just tucked it in the back of my mind and moved on to *Invaders from Mars* and just tried to forget about it. At that point it wasn't available on tape or anything so the only way you could watch it was to go to the theatre and see it there. So I watched it a bunch of times and the end result was that I decided that sometimes they work, sometimes they don't and I just let it go. Lately, however, I think differently. I was in a relationship recently that went really, really bad. So the evening of the termination of this relationship, I went home, not in a great frame of mind at all, and turned on the TV and lo and behold, *Lifeforce* came on. I watched it again and thought…wow…this is one of my favorite films.

There's no other film like it. It really is something special…

It is. And you know, after this woman and I broke up, I realized that *Lifeforce* is really about a relationship between a man and a woman. And when I say that it's one of my favorite films, I don't mean out of the ones I made…I mean it's one of my favorite films, *period*.

Let's talk about one of the main reasons so many teenage boys in the 1980's loved Lifeforce: *Mathilda May…*

Ohhhh, Mathilda!

My God, man, how did you find her?

Well, because it was a large budget, girls flew in from all over London to audition. Some casting agent found this girl in Paris and said, *"Tobe, you have to see her. She's a ballerina, she's 17 and I think she's right for the part.* So we brought her over and I screen tested her and I was like, whoa…it was this perfect look, she couldn't have been better…I wanted her to have a kind of replicant feeling, you know like in *Blade Runner*, but I think she was better than the replicants. And none of them went down to their natural costumes. After 117 shooting days, the lack of costume *was* her costume.

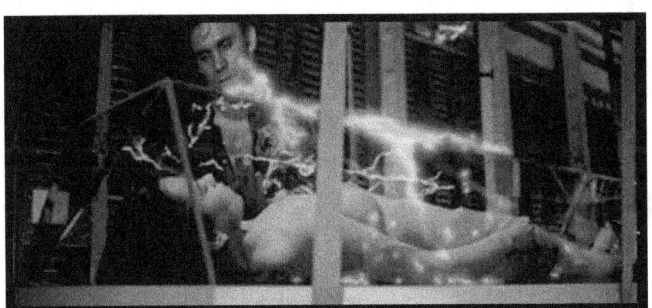

Mathilda May makes for a lethal Sleeping Beauty.

I first saw the film in the shortened American version, with the incredible Michael Kamen music mixed with the Henry Mancini stuff and I have to admit that I think it's a better cut…

After a while, I started liking the shorter version better too…it's tighter.

Was the film taken out of your hands and re-scored?

Not at all. I chose Kamen myself; I went through the entire process. James Horner was originally supposed to score the film and Morricone wanted to do it. Originally I was like, "Why on earth would Ennio Morricone want to do this?" And then, years later, I saw *Bugsy* and thought…ahhh, wow, I get it. It would have been a very different picture if he had. Still, Hank [Mancini] did a great job.

THE LIVING DEAD AT THE MANCHESTER MORGUE
1974

Starring Cristina Galbo, Ray Lovelock and Arthur Kennedy
Written by Juan Cobos, Sandro Continenza, Marcello Coscia and Miguel Rubio
Directed by Jorge Grau

Is there any movie monster more metaphorically rich and viscerally potent than The Zombie? That shambling, moldering imitation of life, that lazy-lidded, pungent shadow of what we once were, a sickening Xerox of humanity whose inherent warmth is replaced by a blind, seemingly limitless lust for slurping the flesh off our still-living bones. The Zombie—a mirror of societal ills and social unrest, a parallel of the have-nots rising up en masse, unstoppable, to devour the unsuspecting haves. The Zombie.

Forged in voodoo lore, crossbred with the vampire by author Richard Matheson and later perfected by undisputed walking stiff maestro George A. Romero, the zombie has endured and evolved in our culture, in cinema, in literature and most recently, in the first person matrixes of our favorite video games.

But for the sake of this essay, let's start our story in Pittsburgh, 1968, with that too-tall, goggle-eyed grandfather of American horror, Uncle George himself. Taking his cues from Matheson's seminal 1954 vampire-plague novella *I Am Legend* ("I ripped him off!" the writer/director unashamedly once told me), commercial/industrial filmmaker Romero's first feature was a nightmarish, grainy, black-and-white tale of undead apocalypse, a gruesome yarn of the fresh dead inexplicably reviving and groping their grey-eyed way to cannibalize the living. That picture, *Night of the Living Dead*, would slowly shamble its way into horror history, becoming a critical and cult favorite, a staple at midnight screenings and a massive international hit, especially in Europe where it was heralded as a Grand Guignol art-house masterpiece.

Enter filmmaker Jorge Grau, a young, experimental Spanish director who, along with an equally visionary, French New Wave inspired pack of bratty celluloid slingers (the likes which include *Blood Spattered Bride* helmer Vincente Aranda) was, at the time, being championed as the avant garde future of the Spanish film industry. In the wake of Grau's violent, sexual and historically accurate telling of the Elizabeth Bathory legend, 1973's *The Bloody Countess*, producer Edmondo Amati approached the filmmaker to direct a movie that would blatantly ride the box-office coattails of the Romero picture, but add the more immediate dimension of dripping, full-blooded color, replacing the gritty, cheap, shadowy expressionism of *Night* with a more garish, pulpy and stomach-churning palette. Grau, swayed by a larger paycheck and the chance to film in England eagerly obliged, taking the rather straightforward genre screenplay and giving it a rewrite, grafting on his own, unique personality quirks, obsessions and style, borrowing from Romero's creation but forging something completely fresh and deliciously offbeat. Known on these shores under at least a dozen lurid (and occasionally ludicrous) titles, including *Don't*

Open the Window, Brunch with the Dead and *Let Sleeping Corpses Lie*, Jorge Grau's blood-freezing 1974 Spanish/Italian zombie shocker *Non Si Deve Profanare Il Sonno Dei Morti*, is a movie that I've always preferred to call by its UK moniker, *The Living Dead at the Manchester Morgue*.

Say it with me:

THE LIVING DEAD AT THE MANCHESTER MORGUE.

See? Doesn't that just sound so much fucking cooler?

London antique dealer George (a bearded, badass-looking Ray Lovelock from, among many other things Armando Crispino's *Autopsy*) is on a cross-country motorcycle trip into rural England when, after a bike-crushing accident, he regretfully hooks up with the beautiful, fragile Edna (Christina Galbo from *What Have You Done To Solange?*) who is also traveling into the sticks to visit her mentally-ill sister. En route, the pair come across a strange machine, a whirring, pulsing metallic engine sitting squarely in the centre of a farmers field; an agricultural device that sends out waves of low frequency radiation designed to provoke insects to go mad and cannibalize each other. Lanky haired, neo-hippie George balks at such underhanded environmental buggery, a position that only increases in intensity when he and Edna discover said supposedly harmless radiation is in fact stimulating the recently dead to get up and kill, with the people they kill then getting up to kill. As the local police (led by the legendary American stage actor Arthur Kennedy, in a cruel and cranky performance) attempt to pin the rash of violent zombie-induced murders on the troubled couple, the evil crop-protecting, dead-provoking device keeps chugging and spinning and the corpses keep-a-coming, resulting in the inevitable tragic, violent, titular morgue-set climax.

When *The Living Dead at the Manchester Morgue* was released it almost immediately came under fire from critics for its then outrageous levels of graphic splatter, a truly shocking cavalcade of carnage designed by none other than Italian FX wizard Giannetto De Rossi. De Rossi is the latex and Karo syrup-slinging genius who would later find acclaim drilling brains, poking out eyes and regurgitating guts under the watchful eye of the late,

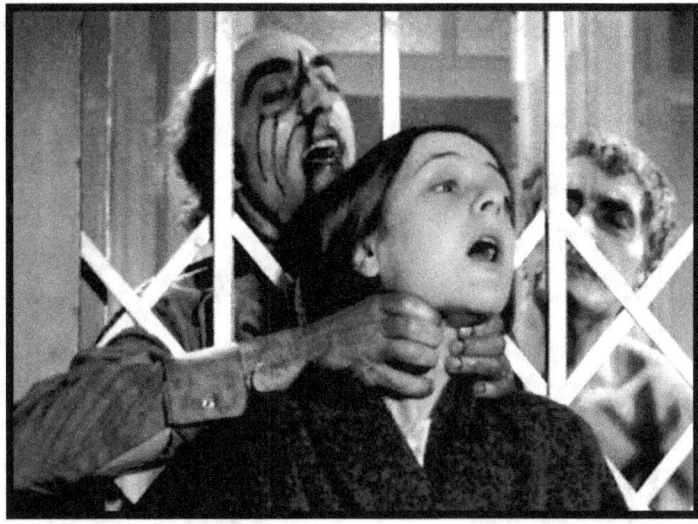

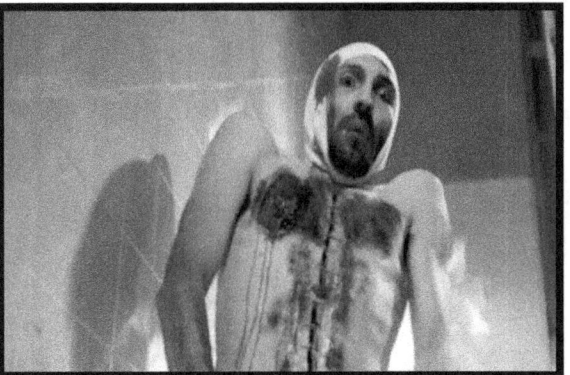

Top: Edna (Christina Galbo) is attacked by zombies.
Middle: One of the *LDATMM*'s hungry, relentless ghouls
Bottom: Italian re-release poster, retitled to pass itself off as a sequel to Lucio Fulci's *Zombi 2*

great Fulci and though his art here was not yet quite state of, it's still pretty damned fantastic: flesh is ripped from bodies, innards are torn out of heaving bellies, eyeballs are eaten and perhaps most notoriously, an unfortunate lass has her blouse ripped open and her left breast crudely removed by the clawing hands of a hungry ghoul.

And speaking of ghouls, the homicidal stiffs on display here are truly terrifying; a mangy, slow and stiff lot of relentless red-eyed refuse (incidentally, the crimson contact lenses appear exactly the same as the ones utilized for the "infected" in Danny Boyle's *28 Days Later* and its sequel *28 Weeks Later*). And these zombies aren't a bunch of amateur local yokels bumbling around

Misleading U.S. poster that piggybacks on *Last House on the Left*'s infamous "It's Only a Movie" ad campaign.

in greasepaint but are in fact real actors, characters ripped right out of the worst (or best, as the case with us horror fans may be) nightmare; I can honestly say that Spanish actor Fernando Hilbeck's gravestone-tossing, recently-resurrected drowned hobo Gutherie, with his sopping wet clothes, blotchy stare and stubbly lock jaw is one of the most frightening screen bogeymen I've ever seen and the damage he inflicts on his victims is just as shuddery.

But beyond the moldy monsters and the ample waste of human life on display, the real impact in Grau's remarkable motion picture lies in the level of intelligence, of finely crafted human drama, of mounting dread and almost Hitchcockian suspense (and black humor) that so effortlessly guides the grue. We come to genuinely care for George and Edna, to believe in their blossoming love, their genuine connection that builds under the direst of circumstances. And when things take a turn for the worse in the final reel, there's a palpable sense of loss that pushes the horror into an emotional level unseen in the post-*Night*, non-Romero zombie efforts. The score by Giuliano Sorgini (*SS Hell Camp*) is another major source of the picture's skin tightening power, a soundscape that deftly veers between string-soaked British-lounge pop (especially effective in the dazzlingly edited opening credits montage) and heaving, gasping, synth burbling experimentalism.

Long available in a pristine, widescreen, 5.1 sound surround edition from Anchor Bay under the less wild title *Let Sleeping Corpses Lie*, *The Living Dead at the Manchester Morgue* is an accessible, thought-provoking and paralyzing Eurohorror classic whose ample flaws, frequent lapses in logic (does ANY of the action actually take place IN Manchester?) and many plot inconsistencies (how does Hilbeck manage to revive his fellow cadavers by wiping blood on their eyelids, exactly? Who cares! It's creepy!) take a backseat to the movie's many macabre and gruesomely elegant delights.

This isn't the quasi-realist American horror of Romero and it isn't the chunky in-your-face zombie opera shock of Fulci. This is the zombie film as dark, lyrical, melancholy fairy tale, a film that exists in a class of its own. In fact, that's a fine word to describe the tragically unprolific Grau's film: Classy.

THE MANY LIVES OF MARK DAMON

November 2008

Some time ago, while perusing the special features on my DVD reissue of Mario Bava's *Black Sabbath* (contained in Anchor Bay's magnificent Bava Box Set Vol. 1), I was pleasantly surprised by the addition of an interview with an actor by the name of Mark Damon. See, I was a rather huge fan of, not only the Bava masterpiece (Damon starred as the young hero in the chilling Boris Karloff episode in *Black Sabbath* called "The Wurdulak") but also of the legendary and groundbreaking 1960 Roger Corman/Poe/Vincent Price creeper *House of Usher* and perhaps even more relevantly, the 1973 soft-core Eurotrash shocker *The Devil's Wedding Night*.

When I was 11, I caught *The Devil's Wedding Night* on late-night pre-teen masturbation staple Elvira's syndicated *Movie Macabre* TV show and was really shaken by it. Director Luigi Batzella's kinky vampire yarn cast a very shaggy and pork chop side-burned Damon as twin brothers on the trail of the mythical Ring of the Nibelungen, a quest that leads them to the doorstep of Countess Dracula herself. Boasting a rich, dark visual palette and bolstered by the intensely erotic presence of Italian horror starlet Rosalba Neri (Anglicized here, as in the previous year's *Lady Frankenstein* as Sarah Bay), the eerie, tacky, ultra-hot (though Elvira's print excised much of the sweatier sex) and bizarre shocker's strongest asset was a rather focused, surprisingly sinister turn by the cruelly handsome Damon, who in a rare bit of head-spinning movie madness, gets the chance here to drive a stake through his own heart.

At any rate, the fascinating supplemental oncamera interview with Damon on the Bava DVD revealed a man who had lead many, many lives, each one more relevant than the last...

Discovered while working in a fairground by the great comedy icon Groucho Marx, Damon found fame as a teen idol in such B-pictures as *Young and Dangerous* and *The Party Crashers* before fate wormed him into the path of young, pulp movie maven Roger Corman. After starring as the foil to Price's haunted nobleman and becoming creatively involved in various projects (including a rather shocking one—to me anyway—revealed in the interview, and detailed explicitly in the following paragraphs below), Damon decided to radically alter his Hollywood life, moving to Italy where he became an icon of the Spaghetti Western (he also introduced the young actor Clint Eastwood to filmmaker Sergio Leone, but again, more on that later) and starred in several gladiator pictures and, of course... a few choice horror movies.

But Damon's serpentine story doesn't end there. After whiling away the better part of the '60s and the early days of the 1970s in Rome, living the high life and submerging himself in Italian film culture (and bedding a fabulous array of Italian women), the actor returned to the U.S. where he almost immediately started the next phase of his life, one which would see him working almost exclusively behind the lens. In the years that followed, Damon has become a major Hollywood player, a mogul, producing such pictures as the Oscar-winning Charlize Theron docu-thriller *Monster* and the upcoming remake of *It's Alive*.

Damon has long claimed he co-directed 1961's *The Pit and the Pendulum*, a claim that credited director Roger Corman disputes.

And although his absolutely riveting autobiography, *From Cowboy, To Mogul, To Monster: The Neverending Story of Film Pioneer Mark Damon* sits on shelves across the world and has been garnering rave reviews, I opted to track Damon down myself and ask him the very personal questions that I selfishly needed to know.

Here we go...

Okay, Mark, right off the top I have to ask you a question that has been burning a hole in my head since I first heard it…

Which is…?

On the supplemental features on the recent Black Sabbath *reissue in the Mario Bava box set, you dropped the bomb that it was you who directed 1961's Roger Corman classic* The Pit and the Pendulum, *and not Roger…*

Well, let me explain that. I took Roger to lunch one day with the plan to wrangle my first important lead in a movie. I said, "Roger I have three books that are in the public domain that I think would make sensational films, in fact they've already been made into films in the past. If I tell you what those books are and if you accept to make them, I want to star in the first and direct the second." Roger said, "Okay Mark what are they?" I told him they were *Fall of the House of Usher, Pit and the Pendulum* and *Masque of the Red Death*. So that day he went to Sam Arkoff and Jim Nicholson and pitched them and they went for it. So I starred in *House* and I was supposed to direct the second but AIP wouldn't accept me as a director. So Roger said, "Listen Mark, you can direct the actors and I'll handle the action and special effects but I can't give you credit, just experience...and my name has to go on it." I was fine with that.

So, in Pit *then, you had the chance to direct one of my favorite genre icons, the irreplaceable British actress Barbara Steele. She, like you, also made a major mark working in Italian films, but what was she like as a person?*

Barbara was sensational. We were really great friends. We never really went to bed together but we got very close at one point and decided that sex would ruin a beautiful friendship. But she really was one the most unique people I've ever known, a truly free spirit, dedicated to her craft and dedicated to having fun. She had a great sense of humor and a great laugh, a completely delicious person…

And then you went to Italy shortly afterwards. I'm a huge admirer of that period in Italian film history and I'm wondering how you ended up in Rome making these wild films…

I went to Rome because Luchino Visconti invited me there to star in one of his pictures, *Boccaccio '70*, which didn't work out. I later found out that the real reason Visconti wanted me there was that he had seen a picture of me winning a Golden Globe and thought I looked very much like French actor Alain Delon. He had been having an affair with Alain Delon and he wanted me to take his place as his lover to make Delon jealous. So he invited me there to star in the film and I ended up hanging out with him a lot. I was kind of a darling with the gay set in Rome for about a year until they realized that I was absolutely straight and wouldn't go to bed with any of them. So ultimately,

I lost the role in *Boccaccio '70* to Tomas Milian, who did go to bed with Visconti after a game of truth we had at a party. Shortly after that, director Sergio Corbucci cast me in a Western called *Johnny Oro*, or as it became known in the U.S., *Ringo and His Golden Pistol*.

How many of these films did you end up making?

I must have made about 15 Westerns, not to mention the handful of sword and sandal, action and horror pictures in Rome, which was strange because I was a very serious young New York stage actor. I even taught acting for a while. So even though I thought these B-films may have been somewhat beneath me, I decided to throw myself into it with great passion. I learned to ride a horse fairly well, learned to sword fight and learned to become an action star. It was a lot of fun.

And you also learned to speak Italian. Are you still fluent or has that left you?

No, I'm still totally fluent in Italian.

Let's talk about The Devil's Wedding Night. *What are your memories of the director?*

The director was me.

I thought the film was directed by Luigi Batzella…

Well, he was the one who put his name on it and called, "action" and, "cut." But when I went into that film, I said I'd only do it if I could direct and he was more than happy to let me. I wrote most of it as well. It was similar to the Corman situation but I was far more active and I basically directed it all. In those scenes when I was playing a twin, he helped by starting the action, but otherwise it was all me. I wasn't really proud of the picture but I had the chance to play twins and that was fun. I think all actors want to do that at some point…

In The Devil's Wedding Night, *you also worked with an Italian actress who pretty much helped define femininity for me as a kid…I'm talking about Rosalba Neri, or as she's known in anglicized prints, Sarah Bay. Tell me about her…*

Ah yes, Rosalba. When I did my first picture with her—I think it was *Johnny Yuma*—I'd flirt with her like mad and laugh so much and we really became great, great friends. She was a bit like Barbara [Steele] really; she had that same vivacious energy. I put her in *The Devil's Wedding Night* because I loved working with her so much. We used to go to all these Italian orgies together, we'd laugh and scratch each other, you know. She made fun of her sexuality. She knew what she was supposed to do as a femme fatale. She milked it. She'd pop her nipples out before scenes began and laugh and call each breast by a name. Outrageous girl. It was all laughs until the camera rolled and then she was all business. And in reality, outside of her vampish behavior, she was really just a woman who wanted to get married and have kids and saw this acting persona as simply a job.

Those days in Rome, at that time…I mean, I heavily romanticize that period as a cinephile but it pains me that I'll never be able to experience it. Those days are long gone but man; it must have been a trip…

Yes that's true, it was incredible and I had a ball, really. I loved it. It was so vibrant, such fun and there was such a sense of camaraderie, especially within the circle of American actors who were living and working there. We called it Hollywood on the Tiber and it was, though it was so much more than that…

What memories do you have about Sergio Corbucci? I love the man's work and find his pictures to be, in certain ways, better and less pretentious than Leone's Westerns...

Less pretentious, yes, and he was also a great comedy director. Corbucci showed me specifically how to do comedy in film, actually. Did you know that we wrote *Django* together?

What? No way!

Yes, we did. We wrote it for me to star in, as a matter of fact. But at the time, I was doing this very high profile picture that went over schedule and I was talking to Sergio every day and he kept saying, "Mark, when are you going to finish!" There was nothing I could do. I was chained to this other film; I couldn't get out of it. So one day he called me and said that he found this boy in a gas station, who looked great, by the name of Franco Nero. So Nero became *Django* and a huge Italian actor. And *Django* is a classic.

How do you think leaving Hollywood affected your acting career in the long run?

It actually doomed my career, towards the end of it. As Westerns went out of fashion, I did as well. They called me a *cappeloni*—a 10-gallon hat, the ones that cowboys wear. I eventually wasn't being seriously considered for other kinds of movies and my career started to grind to a halt as roles became few and far between and money become less and less. That's when I decided to change gears. I met an actress named Margaret Markov—who eventually became Maggie Damon, my wife, during the filming of the movie *The Arena*. I knew that in order to keep this extraordinary woman in the lifestyle that she was accustomed to, I had to make a change. With hat in hand I went to a producer friend of mine and asked to learn about distribution. I knew everyone in Hollywood and the Italians thought I could buy interesting pictures, which I did. I quit acting and have never looked back.

What about Roger Corman. Do you still talk to him?

Oh yes, absolutely. We are both IFTA (Independent Film and Television Alliance) board members and we see each other all the time. You know, he's 82 now and still looks like he's in his early 60s. What an incredible man.

I interviewed him recently and was amazed at how razor sharp his memories of his work were...

Really? Because I was talking to him the other day and found that he had trouble placing dates and events. Not that he wasn't sharp, but he couldn't recollect as much as I could.

What are your thoughts on House of Usher *today? It still gives me chills...*

To hear people say that today still amazes me and I'm delighted. But back than I thought we were putting out a bowl of pablum, just a junk food movie. I guess I was wrong!

Did you have similar feelings about The Devil's Wedding Night?

Absolutely and I'm really amazed that anyone still cares about that movie. In fact all of those films, it blows my mind to learn that many of them are considered cult classics.

MAXIMUM OVERDRIVE 1986

Starring Emilio Estevez, Pat Hingle and
Laura Harrington
Based on the Short Story "Trucks" by Stephen King
Written and Directed by Stephen King

It takes courage to stand up and bravely declare your love for a film that almost every living, breathing person declares to be an absolute atomic bomb. You run the risk of spinning yourself into the roll of cinematic social outcast, shunned by your peers and ridiculed by your pals. But I've never been one to give a gear what anyone else thinks about me so what the hell, here goes:

I fucking love Stephen King's *Maximum Overdrive*. In your FACE!

Yes, *Maximum Overdrive*, the hubcap-headed, gas-spitting 1986 sci-fi action trash classic; the first and—if you believe his publicly uttered promise—*only* film to be directed by master dark fantasy/horror fiction legend King. The film was one of the worst-reviewed studio pictures of its time and it has since been either ignored, reviled or smarmily embraced by pretentious college kids as a pot-enhancing, blissfully bad '80s moron movie experience, on par with real deal dreck like *American Ninja*. And while the diesel-powered shocker is indeed nowhere near a decent creeper and is a pretty odd choice for one of the major forces of literary fear as maiden film voyage, I think it's a fascinating example of the working class hero King aesthetic in full effect and truly believe that there's more going on in the picture than perhaps even its director understood. And at the very least, the movie's chief antagonist is a homicidal, toy-tugging, '70s semi-truck with the grinning image of the goddamned Green Goblin on it. So yeah, there's a trailer load of treasures to appreciate and adore here.

Let's have a look…

As a phantom comet circles the earth, every machine on the face of the planet begins to snap into consciousness and revolt violently against their human makers and masters. Steamrollers level little leaguers, pop machines fire off soda cans into skulls like bullets, electric steak

One of *Maximum Overdrive*'s killer vehicles slips into murderous high gear taking one of many victims for deadly ride.

knives hunger for blood, junkyard wrecks scream to life and monstrous rigs mow down men and women alike. As the world goes entertainingly mad, a ragtag band of shell-shocked survivors congregate at the Dixie Boy truck stop where they unplug, hole up and try to evade the increasingly angry assemblage of evil automobiles.

Maximum Overdrive is based on King's truly eerie early-period short story *Trucks,* which most famously appeared in his bestselling 1978 collection *Night Shift*. I remember sifting through my dad's paperback when I was seven, you know, the one with the eyeball riddled bandaged hand on the cover (an image culled from the story *I am the Doorway*) and, while not as devastating as the *Graveyard Shift, Grey Matter* or *One for the Road* tales, *Trucks* still got me good, especially the final, ominous airplane gazing line. So it's a real head-scratcher why the universally adored author opted to turn that shivery tale into a testosterone-fueled redneck black comedy instead of a straight up genre piece. Many critics in 1986 were asking the same question and needless to say, *Maximum Overdrive* was chewed up and spat out like so many Truckasaurus hors d'oeuvres.

And while much of the maligning is merited, I can't dismiss the film as flat out bad. It has far too much personality for that. Because no matter what your take on this trashy classic, if you know King's universe you'll recognize that the people that populate *Maximum Overdrive* are vintage King creations. We have our reluctant hero, the recently paroled short order truck stop cook (here played by a scrappy Emilio Estevez) who's just trying to live a square life. There's his fat, greasy, abusive boss (Pat Hingle) who exploits him and threatens to send him packing back to prison if he gets out of line. The spunky female hitchhiker (Laura Harrington) who's both sexy and razor sharp under pressure. And there's that cloistered King small town aesthetic, like Norman Rockwell by way of Alfred Hitchcock, that permeates almost every inch of his body of scribblings.

And then there are the trucks.

King would later expand the ideas explored in *Trucks* and shrink their scope in *Christine*, itself adapted for the screen by John Carpenter in 1983. When it came time to turn *Trucks* into *Maximum Overdrive*, King exploited the visual sting of seeing mighty machines marauding and murdering with nary a driver in sight to, well, *maximum* effect. From the opening bridge massacre sequence, *Maximum Overdrive* is a full out orgy of smashed windshields, crunching metal, spinning wheels, blaring horns and splattery human remains. He really went for it and it's grand fun to see chrome crushing people ad nauseum, all cut to the endless strains of AC/DC…

Didn't I mention that AC/DC did the music for this classic?

The beloved Aussie trash rockers were a favorite of King's and he commissioned them to both write the blaring score for *Maximum Overdrive* and lend some of their back catalogue classics to the fold as well. Now, I'm not a huge AC/DC fan but man alive does their evil brand of trucker metal jack this picture up, up, up! Seeing the Green Goblin-faced semi roaring down the streets during the opening credits while the tune "Who Made Who" pounds away in the background is damn near poetic.

Maximum Overdrive is not an art film. It's not meant to be taken seriously. It's not even a horror film really. But King has claimed he wanted to make a junk food movie of the highest order and baby, he succeeded smashingly. Twenty-some-odd years later, *Maximum Overdrive* still has the same brutal, trashy, primal, violent power that pulses away in the background of all of the authors works. It's loud, rough, funny, silly, obnoxious and just plain powerful white trash terror at its redneck, working-class best.

NOMADS
1986

Starring Lesley-Anne Down, Pierce Brosnan,
Anna Maria Monticelli
and Adam Ant
Written and Directed by John McTiernan

In case you haven't noticed, I tend to gravitate towards cinema that isn't necessarily perfect but rather is flawed, fascinating and enigmatic; movies that reflect upon the messy mysteries of the human condition by cloaking their truths in a thin sheen of blood and abstract fantasy. I like films that are hazy, a bit out of focus, tonally out of reach; pictures that you keep revisiting in order to unravel their gauzy secrets. John McTiernan's convoluted 1986 *Nomads* is one such feature. This movie has both followed and frustrated me for years, and I think it's high time that it got some respect.

During a long, graveyard shift in the ER, pretty young Doctor Flax (Lesley-Anne Down) encounters a beaten, bloody man (Pierce Brosnan) who initially appears to be a stark raving-mad transient. When the run-down, sleep-deprived MD leans in to check his pupils, the pair momentarily lock eyes before the wild-eyed lunatic bursts from his gurney, locks his jaw around her neck and whispers something in French before finally collapsing, dead.

Shaken, Dr. Flax is treated for her minor wounds and left to lie down and collect her bearings; almost immediately she begins to experience vivid hallucinations that send her into violent fits. As she soon discovers, the drooling madman that attacked her wasn't a madman at all but rather a famous Canadian anthropologist named Jean Charles Pommier, a man, who after traveling the earth studying nomadic cultures, had finally settled down at the request of his gorgeous wife (the persuasively beautiful Anna Maria Monticelli) into a cushy teaching gig in LA.

Apparently, shortly before his death, Pommier had been tracking a leather-clad gang of street punks (whose ranks include '80s rocker Adam Ant and cult film heroine Mary Woronov) drifting around his home. Turns out these homeless, rootless ruffians are in actuality a tribe of evil, nomadic spirits, the same breed of ancient, wandering souls he'd been obsessively following his whole life and are now hell-bent on driving him mad. The bite that Jean Charles gives Dr. Flax inexplicably causes her to aggressively relive—and we, the audience, along with her—the memories leading up to his final sad state. Soon enough, she too becomes sucked into the Nomads' secret, clandestine, twilight world.

I saw *Nomads* theatrically in 1986 (I bought a ticket for the PG-rated *Back to the Future* and snuck into the R-rated film instead) and I can clearly remember the disorienting effect it had on me. See, *Nomads* doesn't really make much sense, not in a linear, easily digestible way, anyway. The odd narrative structure—with its flashbacks within flashbacks, ever-shifting points of view and lack of clear explanation as to the Nomads' history or true intent—made for a rather infuriating initial viewing experience. But I soon discovered that I could not stop thinking about it. I became obsessed with it. When it arrived on home video months later, I watched and re-

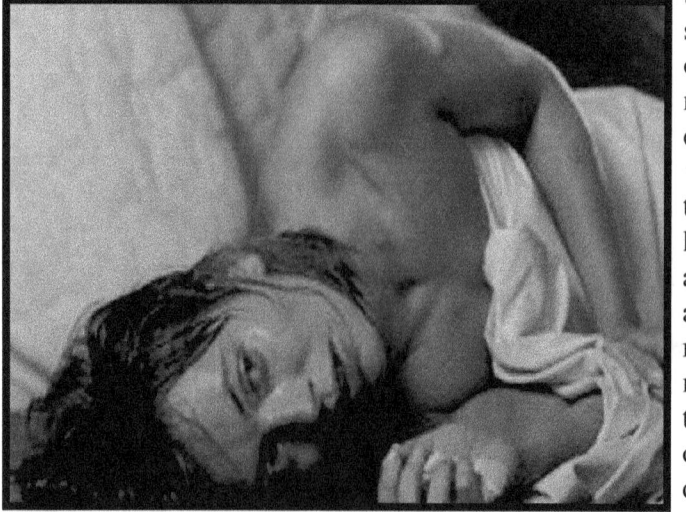

watched it numerous times, trying in vain to decipher its clues and determine what made the movie resonate so much with me.

Today, I still can't properly articulate why I hold *Nomads* in such high regard. I still don't really get it.

But *Nomads* has something. An aura, a lyricism, a kind of poetry. It has that certain—as Pommier himself might say—*je ne sais quoi* that elevates it beyond simple '80s genre potboiler and into the fluid, subconscious realms of the surreal.

I *can* tell you that I absolutely adore Bill (*Rocky*) Conti's urgent, erotic synth and guitar score—especially the opening theme and closing hard rock collaboration with Ted Nugent. I can tell you that both Down and Brosnan are magnetic in a pair of extremely difficult roles that require them to achieve a bizarre sort of character symbiosis. I can tell you that the cold, washed-out look of the film (perhaps the mark of a low budget, perhaps not) is claustrophobic and unsettling in its otherworldly, dim lit way.

It's difficult to believe that McTiernan would go on to create an endless spate of high octane, considerably less challenging, popular action pictures like *Die Hard* and *The 13th Warrior* because his maiden cinematic voyage is a work of such strikingly haunting and original moxie, such an intelligent, sophisticated, offbeat and mysterious psychological/supernatural thriller. Maybe the fact that *Nomads* made about 10 cents at the box office scared McTiernan off from continuing in this daring, metaphysical fantasy vein.

Now, I'm not entirely sure if this is a "good" movie or a "bad" movie but you know what? I don't really care.

I know what I like…and I like *Nomads*. A lot.

Top: Pierce Brosnan can't escape the horror of the *Nomads*.
Middle: Cult actress Mary Woronov (*Eating Raoul*) waxes leggy evil.
Bottom: Lesley-Anne Down gives the performance of a lifetime as the tortured doctor in *Nomads*.

NOSFERATU: PHANTOM DER NACHT
1979

Starring Klaus Kinski, Bruno Ganz and Isabelle Adjani
Written by Werner Herzog
Based on the 1922 Film by F.W. Murnau and the Novel by Bram Stoker
Directed by Werner Herzog

Immortality. We all want it, the chance to defy that black specter of death that equalizes all of us. But to live forever, drifting through time like a ghost, unattached to anything, anyplace…anyone. Hiding in shadows until the earth stops spinning on its axis. The crushing loneliness of it…would it really be worth it?

That's the central driving thematic force behind director Werner Herzog's dark, dreamy full-color remake of the immortal 1922 German expressionist classic *Nosferatu*. A film that, although deeply indebted (sometimes almost scene for scene) to the untouchable original, still manages to evolve beyond its experimental horror roots, taking its frame from Murnau, injecting liberal amounts of melancholy and lyricism and becoming a grand scale testament to the genius of one of our greatest living European directors.

After a string of incredibly successful '70s arthouse favorites, filmmaker Werner Herzog, who alongside trailblazing amateurs Rainer Werner Fassbinder and Wim Wenders, was a major figure in the German new wave movement and was given *carte blanche* from American studio 20th Century Fox to make any picture of his choosing. Correctly acknowledging it as the single most important German film of all time, the director opted to set his sights on remaking Murnau's shuddery unauthorized *Dracula* adaptation *Nosferatu*, shooting both German and English language versions and applying his own unique cinematic aesthetic to the oft-filmed tale of the bloodsucking undead. Unfortunately, at the same time Universal Pictures were also prepping the John Badham/Frank Langella take on the Hamilton Deane stage version of *Dracula* and MGM were launching the post-disco era George Hamilton spoof *Love At First Bite*, both easily accessible and hugely popular. Herzog's operatic, meditative anti-horror film was completely at odds with both the times and Stateside sensibilities and his film, *Nosferatu: Phantom der Nacht* (or *Nosferatu: The Vampire* as it was known in the U.S.), although critically praised by some, got lost in the sanguinary shuffle, deemed by most audiences a pretentious, pointless and scare-free attempt to revisit a picture that was already perfect as is.

Of course, that simply is not the case. Herzog's epic tale of disease, death, love, loss and isolation is in truth probably the most evocative and hypnotic vampire film ever committed to celluloid, full stop.

To fully appreciate the one of a kind wonder of *Nosferatu: Phantom der Nacht* one must first understand the work of its creator, the inimitable Werner Herzog. Born and raised in a remote German mountain village, one completely untouched by technology, young Werner would grow up in an environment two shades shy of the Stone Age, not making his first phone call until he was 14 and not seeing his first film until he was 17. But Herzog had something far better than modern distractions to inspire him. He was surrounded by the beauty of the natural world; mountainous terrain, unforgiving nights and swooning days; green grass, gentle winds and free flowing rivers. Herzog would grow up understanding nature, respecting it and most importantly, he was deeply humbled by it. He understood infinitely that Mother Earth

Klaus Kinski strikes a classic Nosferatu pose.

Dracula's technique could use a little work as he makes love to Isabelle Adjani's comely Lucy.

was an unforgiving mistress, a bitch goddess that could kiss as easily as kill and only a fool would attempt to gain the upper hand against her.

So when life spiraled him towards becoming what he would become, Herzog began making movies that told tales of dangerous eccentrics, heroes and madmen whose sometimes valiant, often vain, efforts to conquer nature result in their ruin. Thing is, Herzog would often choose to film these pictures in the very bowels of the badlands that his scripts painted as treacherous, using locals and natives as extras and often personally teetering on the very destruction he sought to chart. His frequent collaborator, the clinically insane performance artist Klaus Kinski, he of the blond hair, widely-spaced eyes and twitchy lips, would, over the span of five incredible pictures become the extension of Herzog, his dark side, the embodiment of his vice and his irrational desire to perhaps subconsciously cause his own destruction. The two became close friends but also mortal on-set enemies, once even plotting to murder each other behind the other's back (check out the shocking Herzog documentaries *Burden of Dreams* and *My Best Fiend* if you don't believe me). The fact that Herzog would eventually cast his beloved nemesis as the undisputed Lord of the supernatural, a Hell-spawned parasite, speaks volumes about their unique and creatively volatile relationship.

Now, back in the early '20s when celebrated filmmaker F.W. Murnau decided to adapt Bram Stoker's best-selling Gothic horror novel *Dracula* for the screen, he ran into a huge problem: Stoker's widow was very much alive and in possession of both her faculties and the rights to her hubby's estate. And she wanted cash. A lot more cash than Murnau was planning to part with. So Murnau, ever the arrogant brat, got the idea to tweak names and places in the story, changing Stoker's suave Transylvanian Count into a bald, bone-white, taloned freak named Orlock, and went ahead as planned, calling his picture *Nosferatu: Eine Symphonie Des Grauens*. As only a moron would miss this flimsy narrative disguise, the widow Stoker sued the director within an inch of his life, resulting in the courts ordering all prints of the picture to be destroyed. But they weren't and years later some of them surfaced, the film was hailed a lost classic and the rest is horror history.

When it came time for Herzog to make his own tribute to this remarkable picture, the *Dracula* property had lapsed into the public domain, meaning he could call his villain Dracula and change the names and places back to their rightful literary origin. His plot, however, follows the original film's setup verbatim: Jonathan Harker (here played by *Downfall*'s Bruno Ganz) lives in quiet bliss in Virna with his porcelain-skinned wife Lucy (played by the ravishing French actress Isabelle Adjani). One day, Harker's giggling, half-mad boss Renfield (brilliantly played by author Roland Topor, the same Roland Topor who wrote the novel on which Polanski's *The Tenant* was based) sends him on an expedition to Transylvania to sell property to one Count Dracula (Kinski), a long trip he promises will cost the young go-getter plenty of sweat…and blood. Harker leaves his beloved Lucy and begins his serpentine journey to Castle Dracula where, after enduring weeks of endless horror, he discovers his host is in fact a night-crawling, neck-nipping monster. As Dracula packs up his black coffins and heads to Harker's hometown, specifically to sample the wares of his wife, a fever-ridden Harker must escape his tower prison and beat the rat-bringing, plague-carrying vampire to the punch before it's too late.

There's nothing in that synopsis that you haven't read or seen before, but remember, this is Dracula retold by a man who tells tales a bit differently than most. This is Werner Herzog's *Nosferatu*, shot on staggeringly eye filling locations in the Netherlands, filled with impossible beauty, eccentric characters and most importantly an almost overwhelming sadness. The film is, as are all Herzog pictures, free of artifice and special effect save for Kinski's shocking makeup design, cribbed wholesale from the original fiend played by actor Max Shreck. Indeed the first time we see Kinski, his bald, pointy eared, rat toothed visage is shocking, not only because of his terrifying visage but more so by the fact that he's completely at odds with the natural beauty around him. I've fielded many complaints about Herzog's choice to duplicate Shreck's outrageous vampiric visual and I will champion his decision to the grave. This Dracula, for all his hideous otherworldly appearances, is simply another one of the director's dangerous outsiders, a creature who has been blessed and cursed with the secret of eternal life and yet forced to live as an outcast, skulking in rotting tombs, in twilight shadow world, free of any sort of comfort…or love. And this vampire needs love, or rather needs to be loved.

And what of Kinski? Does this slobbering but brilliant lunatic who so viscerally brought the monkey-tossing, delusional Don Lope de Aguirre and the megalomaniacal Fitzcarraldo to screeching life, manage to successfully essay a miserable, attention-starved vampire fiend whose bloodlust is only matched by his despair? Fucking right, he does. Whether glowing in the moonlight, hungrily eyeing a dining Harker or creeping up on the beautiful Lucy, Kinski manages to create a monster that is as pathetic as he is terrifying, a monster who wants to re-join the human race but whose disdain for it keeps him terminally distanced from everything. Witness the climactic scene where a broken hearted Lucy finally invites Dracula to drain her, hoping to drown him in daylight and save her husband's soul. In the original, Max Shreck's Count Orlock simply drinks her dry but here, with Kinski in the role, he vainly attempts to engage in 'normal' lovemaking, clumsily pulling up Lucy's dress, clutching her bosom, sniffing her like a suspicious dog, before she lets him off the hook and just pulls him to her throat. It's an erotic, tragic and macabre sequence and there has never been anything like it onscreen before or since.

There's one paralyzing section in *Nosferatu: Phantom der Nacht* that long ago made it one of my favorite films. As the rat plague brought by Dracula ravishes Virna, killing men, women and children without mercy, Lucy wanders the streets trying to convince the few survivors of the undead menace in their midst. The haunting sounds of Popul Vuh, the progressive rock composer also known as the late Florian Fricke, (a frequent collaborator of Herzog's) drifts across a tableaux of an inevitable death: pigs shit in the street, men try to mate with sheep, children dance with fiddlers, couples make love on the cobblestones and Lucy, dressed in white, raven hair pulled tight in a bun, almond eyes open wide, weaves within it all. A table in the middle of the madness sees handsomely attired men and women dining and drinking, inviting Lucy to sit with them. "We all have the plague," a woman matter of factly says as rats dart in and out from between her legs, "and we want to enjoy every last minute we have left."

A frame later and the people are gone. Their feast now simply a table full of hordes of diseased rats. Chilling and beautiful stuff…

Nosferatu: Phantom der Nacht is Werner Herzog's masterpiece. A moving, haunting portrait of the mercilessness and inevitability of death but also a stark statement about how sometimes a brief life filled with warmth, love, beauty and belonging is better than an endless one filled with nothing but icy night. From the gorgeous cinematography, heart-breaking performances, eerie, unforgettable music and even the quintessentially Herzogian dark humor, this is one of the few motion pictures that benefits from several serious viewings, preferably alone, without a break of any kind. To say it pales beside the original is to miss the point…

PSYCHOMANIA 1971

Starring Nicky Henson, Beryl Reid and George Sanders
Written by Julian Zimet and Arnaud D' Usseau
Directed by Don Sharp

Back in the day, when I was just starting to earn an allowance of some substance, I took a chance and dropped a few hard-earned ducats on what would become a quietly defining motion picture in my life.

That film was director Don Sharp's utterly demented 1971 action/horror opus *The Living Dead*, also known as *The Deathwheelers*, but more commonly worshipped under the sensationalistic moniker *Psychomania*.

Telling the tale of a cocky London biker thug Tom (*Witchfinder General*'s Nicky Henson) and his obsessive quest to learn the secrets of eternal life through violent suicide, *Psychomania* is one of my favorite retro-exercises in British trash cinema. It's ostensibly a biker flick, with the devil-worshipping Tom and his fellow two-wheeled gang bangers (who call themselves, appropriately The Living Dead and wear wickedly designed skull helmets and head to toe, skintight, black leather) raising hell in the city streets. But when the hell-raising turns literal, after Tom strikes a deal with his Satanic butler (played by *The Picture of Dorian Gray*'s George Sanders), kills himself and returns as a hog-riding zombie, things start careening into pure genre mash-up madness. One by one, Tom's followers follow sick suit, rising again as immortal ghouls and blazing trails of terror across the countryside.

Meanwhile, Tom's psychic and sickly rich mother (the great Beryl Reid) rubs her hands and looks for a Devil-defying loophole to send her brutal boy (with whom she has a rather unhealthy relationship) back to the bowels of the "bad place." And then things get weird…

Veteran Aussie-born filmmaker Sharp also spat out one of my favorite early '60s Hammer films, *The Kiss of the Vampire*, and if you know that equally eccentric picture well, you understand that his was not the most restrained of cinematic palettes. A deeper look at his resume reveals that he also helmed the third entry in the original *The Fly* series, 1965's unclassifiable and deeply weird, freak show meltdown anti-sequel *The Curse of the Fly*. The man really had an uncanny knack for taking standard, predictable genre fare templates and turning them into something that simply refused to behave. And God bless him for that.

By the time the exploitation film world spun into the '70s, *Easy Rider*-inspired biker films were *de rigueur* and anticipation of Stanley Kubrick's future-shock youth-gone-wild satire *A Clockwork Orange* was high. Screenwriter Arnaud Dusseau (who also wrote the equally offbeat Spanish/UK chiller *Horror Express*) opted to fuse these headline-ripping hot button issue flicks with the post-*Night of the Living Dead* zombie film and the result was *Psychomania*, a relentlessly groovy cocktail of witchcraft, black leather, campy mass suicides, misty graveyards, slumming actors (I'm looking at YOU, George Sanders!), evil frogs, potent nihilism and John Cameron's brilliant music which is perhaps the single most delirious psychedelic soundtrack of the 1970s.

Outrageous one sheet featuring *Psychomania*'s alternate–and perhaps more appropriate–title

Cameron was a former collaborator of psyche-pop star Donavan and a film composer who, along with his band of specially-selected studio players collectively called "Frog," managed to sculpt one of the trippiest, grooviest, eeriest tapestries of sinister "wah-wah" space rock brilliance ever committed to celluloid. From those first few frames of *Psychomania*, as the members of The Living Dead ride in slow motion in and around a creepy, fog-drenched field called The Seven Witches, Cameron's fuzzy, aural acid trips push the picture into the realms of serious, strange art.

So fantastic is this score and so visceral was its impression on me that it literally set me on a course to create low-tech analog music of my own, something I do to this day for film, television and, ultimately, for my own amusement.

Recently, I rediscovered the goofy, badass glories of *Psychomania* (long lapsed into the public domain and now easily available on home video of every format), thus re-igniting my passion for Cameron's incredible music. Now armed with the power of the internet, I was able to find a tiny UK label called *Trunk* that dug up the score, dusted it off and released the rather hard-to-find soundtrack album on CD, which I of course immediately purchased. The next step though, was to find Cameron himself. The man had seemingly never done any interviews about his fine work on *Psychomania* and seeking him out required much effort on my part.

But find him, I did...

A member of The Living Dead does some PG-rated damage.

Seven Suicides— and they roared back as The Living Dead

AN INTERVIEW WITH COMPOSER JOHN CAMERON

July 2008

When you sat down and watched Psychomania *for the first time, without your score, what were your thoughts about this wacky little movie?*

That it was a wacky movie, yeah! It was really weird and kind of bizarre. But it was definitely a product of late '60s and early '70s low-budget filmmaking; they were trying to put everything in there—rock and roll, zombies, action...but no sex, strangely. Well, none that was visible anyway, most of it was inferred, I suppose...

What was Don Sharp like?

Don was a great action director and he shot really great kinetic sequences that made the movie. All those suicides and wild crashes were fantastic. Don was a really good guy to work with too, not an "airy fairy" sort of guy at all. He simply knew the kind of film he wanted to make and did it.

Your work in this film is so trippy and loose...I presume it was mostly improv?

It was mostly written, actually. I tend to write everything when I compose, even guitar parts. But I did give the band some space to be loose. We recorded the music at Shepperton Studios, which is this big old studio designed and used primarily for symphony orchestras. We even had an engineer who still wore a suit and tie to the sessions! Now, a lot of the nature of that score was down to the fact that there were no Moogs avail-

83

*Psychoman*ia has it all—devil-worshipping, chopper-riding zombies just looking for a good time.

able to us. I mean, there were Moogs but they were the size of a house and impractical to transport. So we took guitars, vibes and different instruments and did a kind of Phil Spector thing by putting them through different speakers and phase units. We had to find ways to make weird sounds without synthesizers and this produced was an ingenuity that you don't see nowadays.

For a long time, before it was released to CD, the score was thought to be lost. Who had the masters?

I think Johnny Trunk must have found those but I presume the film studios would have had the masters. Actually, it's quite possible that with *Psychomania* all there would have been was a quarter-inch master. Once it got to be like, 1974, 1975, everybody making movies used multi-tracks for music. But in those days, especially in those cheaper British movies, everything went straight from quarter-inch onto 3-track-dubbing optical prints.

I read once, many years back that Geoff Barrow from the band Portishead *was a big fan of your work on* Psychomania *and partially sculpted his group's signature sound on the main theme. Did you know that?*

Uh…No. Wow.

Has anyone else through the years mentioned how important your score was to them?

Not really. It was only after the CD came out and Johnny Trunk told me about different DJ's doing remixes on the main theme that I became aware of any interest in it. And then, of course, the internet has made me aware of it too…

Starring Anthony Perkins, Diana Scarwid and Jeff Fahey
Written by Charles Edward Pogue
Directed by Anthony Perkins

"There is no God!"

So screameth fallen Sister Maureen, who kneels before an illuminated statue of the Virgin Mary, desperately pleading for guidance, for a sign that God does in fact exist. Over the next 90 minutes, the narrative that slowly unfolds before both her and us, the audience, will provide an answer, albeit a cold, empty and ultimately tragic one.

Yes, Maureen, there IS a God.

And his name is Norman Bates.

For as the lost ex-nun wanders through the desert to the melancholy strains of Carter Burwell's lilting title theme, towards the black, beaten-down haunted palace that is the Bates Motel, it is clear that Charles Edward Pogue's script for the Anthony Perkins-directed sequel *Psycho III* has a metaphorical agenda, one with more than just kinky thrills and second-reel shocks on its morbid mind.

Released theatrically in 1986 to generally dismal critical notices (except the great Roger Ebert who liked the picture almost as much as I do), *Psycho III*, though it boasts its fair share of graphic skin-ripping violence, was at odds with many of its mid '80s slasher flick contemporaries in that it favors atmosphere, allegory and character over a running time-padding body count. The movie is profoundly aware that it hasn't a hope in matching or exceeding the import of Alfred Hitchcock's groundbreaking 1960 black comic nail-biter classic and has little interest in following in the footsteps of Richard Franklin's rather pedestrian 1982 effort *Psycho II*. It instead elegantly mounts itself as a Tennessee Williams-esque musing on the desperate lives of a pack of profoundly lost, achingly downtrodden people who, like many of us, are just looking for an exit. And of course, there's plenty of nudity, blood and homicidal transvestitism thrown in, just to balance the scales.

Now, then. The plot…

Reeling from a botched suicide attempt that results in the death of her Mother Superior, disgraced bride of Christ Maureen Coyle (Diana Scarwid) packs a suitcase and hits the road to nowhere. Her aimless travels lead her to the dilapidated but still functioning Bates Motel, the legendary road stop inn run by recently released cross-dressing, mother-obsessed psychopath Norman Bates (once again essayed by the inimitable Tony Perkins).

When we last saw Bates in *Psycho II* (this film takes place one month after the climax of that picture), he was legally sane and attempting to re-adjust to normal life. Of course, certain people, still bitter over events from the first installment, did their best to drive poor Norman mad anew and succeeded smashingly. Now the twitchy, aging corduroy blazer-wearing lunatic lives a quiet life of simmering but stabilized dementia with his newly stuffed, completely dead, still perched-in-the-window mother. That is, until the damaged Maureen strolls into town.

A ringer for Marion Crane, Janet Leigh's untimely shower-slaughtered victim in the original (they even have the same monogram), Maureen's blonde, wispy presence sends Norman swirling into a neurotic tailspin, the projected voice of his desiccated matriarch urging him endlessly to just, "kill the whore." He reluctantly obliges, finally donning mom's duds and sneaking into cabin one, butcher blade in tow only to uncover the troubled Maureen lying in a tub of her own blood, red-stained razor by her side, wrists still pumping fluid. As her self-destructive lifeforce ebbs, she imagines the wigged, frocked Bates to be the Blessed Virgin and, after Norman opts to drive her to the hospital, thus saving her life, the girl becomes fixated by the notion

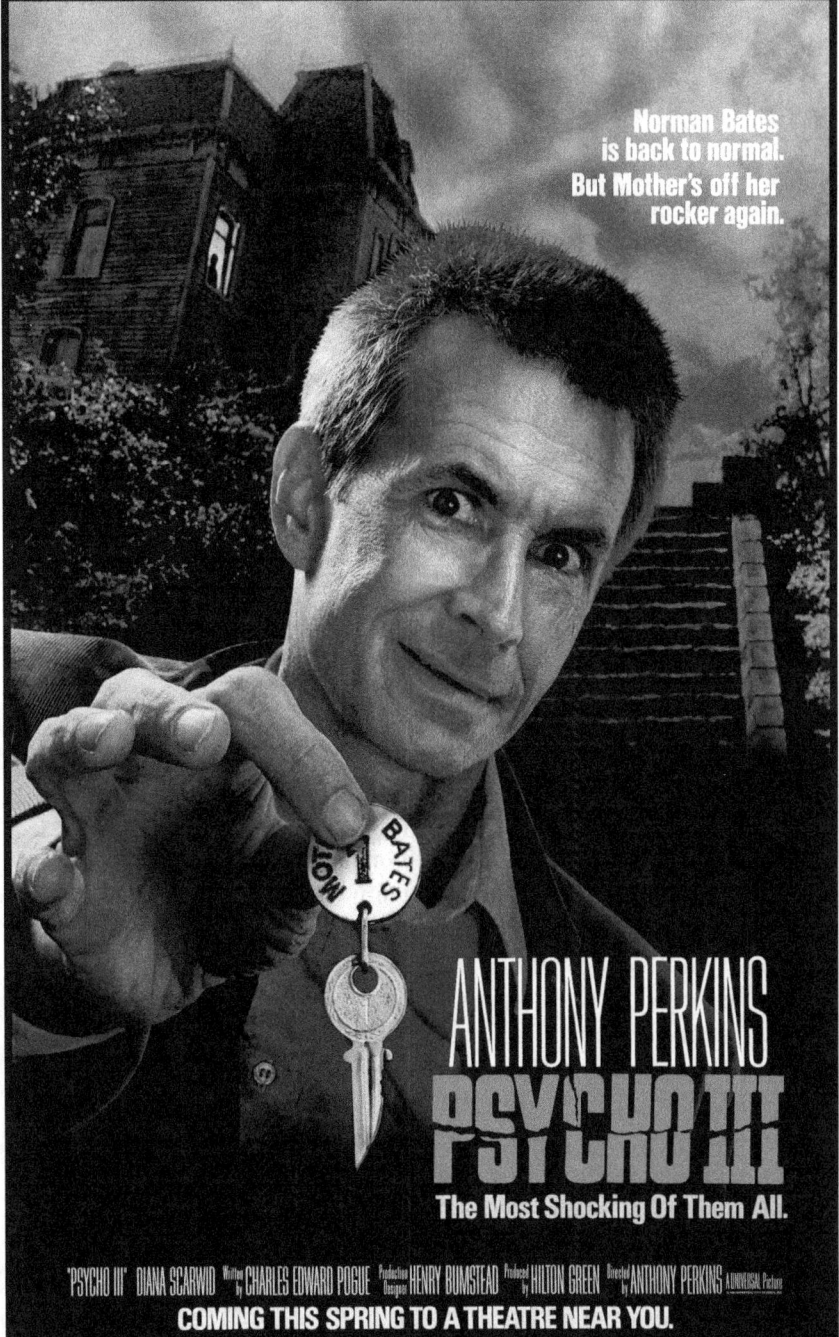

that the serial killer is her savior, her light at the end of long, dark and troubled tunnel. As their ensuing, awkward and childish romance evolves, Norman's new employee, a greasy drifter named Duke (a stubbly Jeff Fahey at the top of his scumbag game) and a tireless female tabloid reporter (*The Changeling*'s Roberta Maxwell) are keeping their eyes on the madman, waiting for him to buckle. And buckle he does, of course…

Psycho III marks the directorial debut of the eternally typecast Perkins (who by this point must have signed on as Bates with the contract clause that he would only do it if he could be boss behind the lens) and truly, he does an outstanding job here. Reverently tipping his hat to his master, Perkins' picture is indeed ripe with the same shuddery, off-color shock humor that marked Hitchcock's best work (Hitch himself often confessed that *Psycho* was intended as a ghoulish comedy); witness the scene where amiable yet obtuse Sheriff Hunt (Hugh Gillin, reprising his role from *Psycho II*) vehemently defends Norman's honor while absentmindedly huffing ice from the ice machine, his fat fingers narrowly missing the butchered

believe the film works incredibly well as a meditative, meandering mood piece and sneering growl against the folly of blindly following an organized religion. For what is our doomed heroine Maureen if not a human pinball, crushed by the oppression of the church and yet still foolishly seeking some kind of messiah, a reason outside of herself for existing? In fact, I find the off-kilter relationship between her and Bates to be the single most interesting element of ANY of the *Psycho* films, the most real, the most human.

spoils of a recently dispatched female victim while repulsively (and hilariously) scarfing down the blood-dripping cubes (and licking his fingers no less!). But again, Perkins and screenwriter Pogue (he of Cronenberg's *The Fly*) are far less concerned with imitation than they are at observing the patterns of hearts without hope. And when *Psycho III* really works, it's because the filmmakers are walking beside Bates, dragging him out of the shadows and studying him out in the open, somewhat sympathizing with his deranged plight, even as he drags his blade across the exposed throat of yet another unwitting woman.

See, the tragedy of Norman Bates—and make no mistake, Bates IS a tragic figure—is that he is, at his core, a good person. Yet so fractured is his fragile psyche from years of protracted childhood abuse that his mind has essentially split (much like the famous Saul Bass title treatment) leaving him at constant war with himself and the grim, torturous reality of his hopeless situation. In *Psycho III*, it's clear that Norman is fully aware of his madness, with the notion that the thing he calls mother doesn't necessarily exist outside the parameters of his perception. But, exhausted after years of keeping her blood-hungry presence at bay, he has simply resigned himself to accepting her, living with her and thus drowning in his own lethal, sexual psychosis.

Now, down to brass taxes: Is *Psycho III* a good film?

Well, much like Dr. Fred Richmond explains in the denouement of the original, yes…and no. I

**Top: Anthony Perkins will forever be cuffed to his role as Norman Bates.
Bottom: Siren Ruthie (Kay Heberle) before she kisses Bates' blade.**

I'm also in love with the look of this picture, the dusty, John Ford-esque landscapes captured by cinematographer Bruce Surtees are breathtaking and, coupled with that delicious Carter Burwell score, push the picture squarely into an arthouse horror territory. But admittedly, what damages the movie and what depressingly prevents it from becoming what it might have been is the cheap, ineffective but obligatory '80s gore and gratuitous nudity. I can't believe I'm saying this but the useless boobs and open wounds really hurt the picture, cheapen it, drag it down into low-rent *Friday the 13th* territory when it clearly cries to be something more evolved.

There's one sequence in *Psycho III* that, for me, summarizes not only what is truly wonderful about the movie, but is one of the most lyrical scenes in the history of horror movies, period:

After the opening credits, when the camera fades into the motel and the tumbleweeds roll and the dust blows and the wind hisses, the camera pans up, up, up the hill to the Bates house. We see a birdfeeder and the various lovely winged creatures that are drawn to it, like the pretty things that have, in the past, gravitated towards the motel itself.

Suddenly a finch gets woozy, flapping its wings, shaking its head and dropping to the ground, convulsing in death. Then a blackbird follows suit, a sparrow soon after. The shadow of Norman Bates creeps into frame over the feathered, obviously poisoned bodies, and he then gently, tenderly, collects his feathered victims and places them in a brown paper bag.

The next scene sees Norman in his kitchen engaging in his favorite pastime (outside of murder), taxidermy. As he cuts open the belly of one dead bird, he scoops a preserving powder with a spoon into its hollowed out frame, the same spoon that he immediately dips into a jar of Peter Pan peanut butter and uses to spread the very same peanut butter onto a Ritz cracker before eating it.

From the corner of his eye, Bates sees the paper bag move. Both he and we believe it to be a twitch of his polluted imagination. But it's not. It's a bird, an inexplicable survivor of the hunt. Delighted, Bates cradles the fragile creature and smiling, opens his back door and sets it free. As the bird flies into the sky, we see a look of such calm, such sweetness across Norman's face.

In less than five minutes, Perkins deftly defines the character that had dogged him his entire professional life, right up until his death of AIDS in 1992.

Child. Victim. Killer. Saint. Ladies and Gentlemen, I give you...Norman Bates.

RAVENOUS 1999

Starring Guy Pearce, Robert Carlyle, Jeffrey Jones and David Arquette
Written by Ted Griffin
Directed by Antonia Bird

If it's true that you are what you eat, then Colonel Ives is every man.

Literally. He's EVERY man.

Because Colonel Ives is a cannibal.

Allow me to speak of Colonel Ives, about his adventures in superhuman flesh eating and the terror and unexpected hilarity that ensue. Come with me as I muse on a film that escapes many a genre film fan's radar and yet has held a very special place in my spleen since I first bore theatrical witness to it way back in 1999.

Now then. Who's hungry?

Me? I'm *Ravenous*.

Directed by British art house filmmaker Antonia Bird (the spectacular dark melodrama *Priest*) as a last

Colonel Hart (Jeffrey Jones) prepares a grisly dish.

Colqhoun (Robert Carlyle) and Boyd (Guy Pearce) do the dance of death.

minute sub for director Milcho Manchevski, *Ravenous* is, simply put, one of the strangest studio-supported shockers ever made. Starting as a kind of Western and then becoming a horror film before revealing itself as a comedy, then a social satire, then a Western again, sliding back into horror before…oh balls, I'm losing you. Let's back up a bit…

Memento vet Guy Pearce stars as Captain Boyd, a soldier who, after playing dead during a Mexican ambush, inadvertently drinks the blood of a slain comrade, gets an inexplicable jolt of energy and single-handedly saves the day. When details of his initially cowardly exploits sour his reputation, he's stationed in the most remote outpost in California, Fort Spencer, a camp populated by assorted drunks, hookah smokers and military castoffs of every sort. One night, a barely dressed, shivering and raving traveler drifts into camp named Colqhoun (*28 Weeks Later*'s Robert Carlyle), spilling a wild-eyed story about his trapped companions and the cannibalistic means they were forced into by their guide, a one Colonel Ives. The outpost leader Colonel Hart (played by the always entertaining Jeffrey Jones in a turn that would be sort of reprised in the awesome HBO series *Deadwood*) in a fit of outrage decides to take leave for the grim site in hopes of rescuing any non-entrée survivors there may be left. However, upon their arrival, it becomes clear that Colqhoun is not only insane but is in fact the demonic Colonel of his own tale; the rescue mission turns out to be a trap and the feral Colqhoun/Ives proceeds to kill and eat as many of the search party as possible. The woozy Boyd—who by this time is fascinated and tempted by the power of cannibalism—tries to escape by jumping off a cliff with the corpse of a semi-chewed colleague. Trapped in a hole, battered and broken—and hungry—Boyd opts to power up and have a bite before setting forth to get his revenge on the maniacal Ives. And then *Ravenous* really gets weird. Turns out the overly virile Ives has tapped into the power of the Wendigo, an ancient Indian cannibal spirit, and has become a sort of superhuman vampire. It becomes clear that his chief goal is to position the apprehensive Boyd as his male Eve, the other half of a soon-to-be-flourishing mid-century skin-eating California über-clan.

Taking its cues from the tragic, true-life tale of the Donner Party (an unfortunately real band of 19th-century settlers that were forced to cannibalize their dead during a treacherous trek), *Ravenous* goes off the rails fairly quickly and refuses to behave by any sort of narrative rule. I think it was this very tonal freestyling that doomed the picture to a critical death, as many journos and genre fans didn't get what Bird and company were trying to do. Now, I can't very well claim that I do either, but I can tell you that *Ravenous* is one of those rare films that stands tall in its staggering originality, a film that defies audience expectations at every turn and manages to entertain smashingly while provoking goosebumps and giggles. You know you're in for a sneering anti-mainstream epic before the word *Ravenous* even pops up onscreen as two portent dripping pre-credits quotes appear: The first is a serious-minded scribble from Nietzsche; the second is credited to Anonymous…it reads, in bold caps, "EAT ME." Incredible stuff…

The cast is universally excellent. Pearce is vulnerable and tough when he needs to be, while Jones and the often-aggravating David Arquette offer fine, quirky turns. But the real star is Carlyle. Looking like a spooked deer one second, turning into a drooling, cunning, salivating wolf the next, the veteran Scottish character actor's onscreen presence as the arrogant ghoul Ives is unlike anything previously essayed by anyone in any film.

In my essays, I always attempt to isolate and stress how pivotal a picture's music is, especially in the annals of horror, to effectively stamp the filmmakers imagery and ideal into your psyche and the score for *Ravenous* ranks as the most unique and effective since Goblin's prog rock in *Suspiria*. Brit rock band Blur front man Damon Albarn and (my personal favorite modern composer) Michael

Nyman have created a disorienting, weird aural landscape of hillbilly loops (Albarn's stuff) and dread-drenched orchestral string stings (Nyman) that uncomfortably combine to goose the already disturbing and outrageous flesh-eating cowboy setpieces and elevate them into brain-scrambling hysterics. The final piece, which meanders over a long, ultra-violent 15-minute struggle between the reluctant Pearce and the cocksure Carlyle, is particularly effective and hypnotic, brilliantly at odds with the frenetic onscreen action.

Full of left field Nietzsche-esque flesh-eating super-man philosophy, gruesome bloodletting, berserk performances, peculiar plotting, deranged music, beautiful cinematography (by Anthony Richmond, *Tales From the Hood*) and a deliciously cross-eyed sense of lunatic humor and bitter satire, *Ravenous* is a fascinating one-off and I'm willing to bet, a future cult classic. And the film may seriously tempt your inner cannibal: one look at that chunky "fork or spoon" human stew bubbling away in the movie's final reel made me fucking ravenous indeed.

THE SENTINEL
1977

Starring Cristina Raines, Chris Sarandon and
Burgess Meredith
Written by Jeffrey Konvitz and Michael Winner
Based on the Novel by Jeffrey Konvitz
Directed by Michael Winner

What are horror films but morality tales whose serpentine roots lie deeply grounded in campfire ghost stories, myth, folklore, fairy tale…and, of course, in theology. Organized religion has almost universally employed narratives of fear and terror as warning signs to obey the rules and exist divinely, to avoid the pitfalls of base temptation and vice lest ye be tossed into the bubbling cauldrons of Hell itself. And since Edison first ran his one-reel *Frankenstein* through his Kinetoscope, this pious, raw, stripping down of elements both spiritual and corporeal have exemplified the best efforts our beloved genre has to offer.

Now, as any good student of recent history should know, the 1960s were a time of change in America, of social and political upheaval. With JFK getting his noggin shattered on live television and the bloody shadow of the Vietnam conflict looming large, the people—fresh out of the pastel perfect 1950s—were no longer blindly trusting of their flag, of themselves…or of their God.

Right and wrong became blurry. Black and white dissolved into various shades of grey. Good didn't always conquer evil and sometimes The Devil would win and there was nothing your endless bible-to-bosom clutching could do about it. As the '60s oozed into the '70s, Americans were shell-shocked. They began to seriously question their previously unchallenged beliefs and, as mainstream pop culture began to reflect this disenfranchisement, so then did horror movies become more morally checkered, delivering the bleakest, most nihilistic answers imaginable.

So too then, were the streams of guarded religious idealism attacked with profitable and controversial relish. This cycle of irreverent, theological-based terror started in 1968 with Roman Polanski's adaptation of Ira Levin's bestseller *Rosemary's Baby*; it went sexually rabid with Ken Russell's depraved 1971 melodrama *The Devils*; it perfected itself with William Friedkin's 1973 classic *The Exorcist* and it climaxed with the operatic pulp of Richard Donner's 1976 shocker *The Omen*. But one picture that sought to ride this potentially blasphemous wave got lost in the shuffle, coming out after films about the persuasive power of The Devil were popular, receiving its cinematic communion perhaps a wee bit too late. Though many people that saw it theatrically back in 1977 still cite it as one of the scariest movies ever made, for whatever reason *The Sentinel* has kind of, sort of just…disappeared.

Allow me to revive it…

Pity poor Alison Parker (the lovely Cristina Raines, daughter of Claude), beautiful model and actress by day and nail-biting nervous wreck by night. As a teenager she accidentally stumbled upon her father engaging in a lurid threesome with two rather rotund whores and, after being beaten by her old man for the intrusion, promptly dragged a razor blade across her own wrist. Though she survived the bungled suicide, years later she tries again after her lover's wife, who, upon discovering her hubby's infidelity, jumps from a bridge to her own emotionally devastated demise. Again, Alison lives through it. Now shacked up with said lover, a slightly sinister high-priced lawyer named Michael (*Fright Night*'s Chris Sarandon), the terminally tortured starlet feels she seriously needs some independence and space to figure out who she is and rents an apartment in a looming NYC brownstone.

Things get weird from the get-go. First off, the far-too-friendly real estate agent (a grinning Ava Gardner) quotes the pad at an already low $500 per month, and casually lowers it another hundred after the not-so-wealthy Alison turns it down. Unfazed by the agent's inexplicably desperate attempts to fill the gorgeous flat, she moves in and is almost immediately visited by a slew of eccentric, almost otherworldly neighbors. There's the doddering old Mr. Chazen (the great Burgess Meredith), a charming oddball who throws birthday parties for his pets; the stuttering old lady who keeps muttering "black-and-white cat, black-and-white cat;" the leering, kinky lesbian dancers (a still-sultry Sylvia Miles and a young and yummy Beverly D'Angelo) who are prone to impromptu tea time masturbation sessions; and then there's the blind, mute and seemingly senile Father Halloran (John Carradine), who does nothing more than sit in the top window and stare through sightless eyes at the world below.

Alison, already teetering on a breakdown, takes this array of oddballs with a grain of salt…until of course she learns that none of them—save the old Priest—actually exist in the natural world. As it turns out, this is no ordinary Brooklyn Heights low rise, but is rather a portal to Hell, a gateway guarded by Halloran and monitored by the Church and the quirky neighbors are in fact evil

ghosts, demons, whose morbid task lies in encouraging Alison to kiss that blade to her vein once again…this time for keeps.

Why?

Well, if I told you that I'd be a real dickhead, wouldn't I? Let's just say, that the eternally put-upon lass learns that she is in fact stuck dead center in a high stakes tug of war between Heaven and Hell and her very soul hangs in the balance. There. Spoiler-free.

The Sentinel is one of the strangest horror films of the 1970s. First of all it was indeed directed by rough and tumble ex-pat British action filmmaker Michael Winner (he of, among other things, the Chuck Bronson vigilante classic *Death Wish*) and Winner's more exploitive, direct, unaffected approach to the material is jarring, at odds with the baroque locations and subject matter. And his casting of high class Hollywood veterans, second only to *The Love Boat*, is absolutely, gleefully loopy. I mean, where else can you see future *National Lampoon's Vacation* mama D'Angelo sharing space with old pros like Meredith, Gardner, Miles and even Eli Wallach (whose work here as a jaded, relentless detective is superb) while furiously rubbing her leotard sheathed clitoris to orgasm? The ultimate aim of Winner's approach is to create a glossy world of high fashion, modern, urban lifestyles, grinning, seemingly benign characters and stuffy clergymen...then take a big old ladle of wet, bloody, grimy sleaze and just smother the whole picture with it like some class of celluloid poutine. Contrary to how that reads, this is NOT a bad thing. Quite the opposite. It's this very tonal dichotomy that gives the film much of its fingerprint.

Upon its release in 1977, *The Sentinel* was not only a tad too late out of the God-fearing gate; it did something that similarly spelled the career death of filmmaker Tod Browning 35 years earlier. In the movie's nightmarish climax, when the demons reveal their true natures and creep out from underneath the stairs, pushing our heroine past the edge of sanity, a cavalcade of real-deal disfigured people joins the already introduced heavies. We see men with facial tumors so extreme and hideous they make John Merrick look like Tom Selleck by comparison. We see thalidomide-damaged women, dwarves, cleft-palated children and at least one poor soul whose lips are so heavy with cysts that they hang like mud flaps from

his drooping mug. When the audience is treated to this parade of damaged people, *The Sentinel*, which until this point is still anchored firmly in fantasy, is dragged into the realms of exploitive reality. Aforementioned director Browning's 1932 classic *Freaks* was a film that similarly sported a cast of disabled and distorted men and women, a move that repelled audiences and almost single-handedly demolished a once-promising career. *Freaks*' notorious reputation has long since been exonerated due to the fact that the various deformed men and women are sympathetic characters, heroes in fact. In *The Sentinel* however, Winner is callously throwing them onscreen in their natural state, without a shred of makeup, and positioning them as agents of Satan, as monsters, as evil, bloodthirsty ghouls. Was it a sensitive move? Probably not, and Winner's credibility was called into question by audiences and critics alike. But whatever your thoughts on this crass casting decision…it works. It really works and the picture is that much more unsettling for it.

There is also some debate as to the shadowy morality of the film (and the book from which it was culled) in that the Catholic Church seems almost as sinister and manipulative as the dual-faced devil himself. The fact that an obviously deeply disturbed young woman like Alison has but one choice to save her soul (remember, Catholics believe suicide to be one of the ultimate spits in the face of God) and that is to essentially give up her identity is upsetting and depressing. She's basically fucked no matter which deity she chooses to succumb too. This is far more exploitive a picture than *The Exorcist* or even *The Omen*, but it's without question the angriest and cruelest and goriest of the bunch.

Ah yes. The gore...

Those who have not seen *The Sentinel* will be pleasantly shocked by the unflinching level of gruesome action on display, much of it courtesy of *The Exorcist*'s Dick Smith. From splitting, blood-spurting heads and cannibalism to the show-stopping scene where Alison bisects an eyeball and hacks off the nose from the reanimated corpse of her abusive father, this pic pushes its R-rating around like a schoolyard bully, cramming in as much wince-inducing nastiness (not to mention skuzzy sexuality) as a 95-minute mainstream '70s Hollywood horror flick can contain. This is delightfully vulgar stuff, friends. If you're a fan of Italian horror, try to see the countless ways in which the great Lucio Fulci quotes this film in his 1981 masterwork *The Beyond*. And if you are indeed familiar with that magnum opus, note the last shot of *The Sentinel* and tell me old man Lucio didn't prick up his ears and scribble some notes...

When *The Sentinel* was released, the Vietnam war was long over, disco was still king, Americans had recovered from, and come to terms with, their collective spiritual abyss and, the empty, coke-fueled, morally bankrupt, superficial 1980s were just a heartbeat away. This, coupled with the general lack of audience interest in *The Sentinel*, not to mention the mini-controversy surrounding its sideshow-tinged climax, started Michael Winner on an unfortunate creative collision course that he never really recovered from. By the time Bronson wooed the director back for the successful yet ugly, cheap, mean and critically maligned sequel *Death Wish 2* in 1982, the aging filmmaker's reputation as B-level hack had been secured. Shame that. Because *The Sentinel* is probably the best film of Winner's expansive career: a solid, disturbing, sick, often campy and occasionally unspeakably horrifying theological mystery ripe with cheap, visceral thrills. With its mismatched, once-in-a-lifetime cast (the likes of which also include the late Jerry Orbach and brief turns by the impossibly young Jeff Goldblum and Christopher Walken) and its cynical, jaundice-eyed view of both Catholicism and society at large it is perhaps the last great intelligent theological horror film of the 1970s.

The Sentinel, quite simply, stands alone.

AN INTERVIEW WITH DIRECTOR MICHAEL WINNER

August 2008

When did Jeffrey Konvitz's novel first land on your radar?

I received a copy of the book after attending a Beverly Hills party thrown by Herb Jaffe where Ned Tanen, then the head of production at Universal Pictures, was also a guest. We talked about the book and he later sent it over to my hotel. Universal had attempted a number of scripts based on it when the novel came out in hardcover but none of them were well liked. By the time I got involved, the book had come out in paperback and was doing very well. They offered me the job of writing a new script and, if they liked it, to produce and direct the movie.

One of the most striking things about the film is the who's who of Hollywood legends cast in sinister roles. How did you manage to get all of these incredible performers involved?

Well, it's simple: they liked my script! But they were all fantastic, really. Burgess Meredith was a professional and a pixie-like delight. He and I became great friends afterwards. Ava Gardner also became a great friend and I saw quite a bit of her in London, where she lived until the day she died. Many of the other actors like Eli Wallach and Martin Balsam had worked with me before...

For your male lead, you had Chris Sarandon, who was at his peak of career. Was he your first choice?

Oh no. I should have had Christopher Walken in the lead instead of the small part he ended up playing but it was Universal that wanted to have Chris in the role. I actually offered the part to Martin Sheen, but to my surprise, the studio said, "We don't want Sheen. He's in television!" Ridiculous.

The Sentinel *is really gory for an R-rated film. Did you have to make any cuts?*

No, the film wasn't censored at all, believe it or not. But yes, it was gory. In a number of interviews, Beverly D'Angelo was asked about the scene where she and Sylvia Miles were eating Chris Sarandon's brains. She told them that I said, "Darling, you'll be with two Academy Award-nominated actors while you're doing it, so don't worry!" It was a jolly picture indeed!

You kind of pulled a Tod Browning by using real freaks for the picture's disturbing climax. Why did you decide to go that route?

I decided to use the real freaks to save hours and hours of prosthetic makeup work, in fact. But they were all very lovely people and greatly enjoyed being in the film. I have a news clipping from a U.S. paper where one of them was being interviewed after the film wrapped and said, "I was so happy to discover that there were other people as deformed as I am and to be with them." His nurse said he viewed it as the single greatest experience of his life. The only thing that was appalling about the whole situation was that the New York crew, who, having worked with the freaks all day, refused to eat with them. So screens were put up to hide the freaks from the crew. It was dreadful, just dreadful. That said, I myself had lunch in my cool, comfortable air-conditioned room. I'm very ashamed I did that. I should have set an example.

THE SOUND OF SHOCK: A BRIEF HISTORY OF CANADIAN COMPOSER PAUL ZAZA

August 2006

Paul Zaza is sitting across from me at a chi-chi bistro in downtown Toronto. We're having lunch. He's buying. I order the hamburger, mostly because I can't pronounce any of the other menu items. He's picking at some kind of chicken dish.

And if the name Paul Zaza means nothing to you, I can most assuredly say it means plenty to me. He is, after all, Canada's answer to Ennio Morricone and I've had my radar honed in on his sound since I was a kid.

Back then, when I was but a snot-nosed tot, I would expose myself to virtually every horror picture I could get my hands on. My father was musical and I was trained from an early age to recognize the importance of music and it's relationship to image. But my relationship with the work of Paul Zaza began with a cable TV screening of *Hello Mary Lou: Prom Night 2*, director Ron Oliver's in-name-only sequel to the Jamie Lee Curtis horror hit. The film was a kind of sexploitational cross between *The Exorcist* and *Carrie* and was one of those flicks that even at the age of 12, I knew was pretty rank...but I dug it all the same.

One of the things that really drove the onscreen nonsense for me was the ominous, string-scraping score. I did some research that summer on the man that both composed and performed that music and found out that

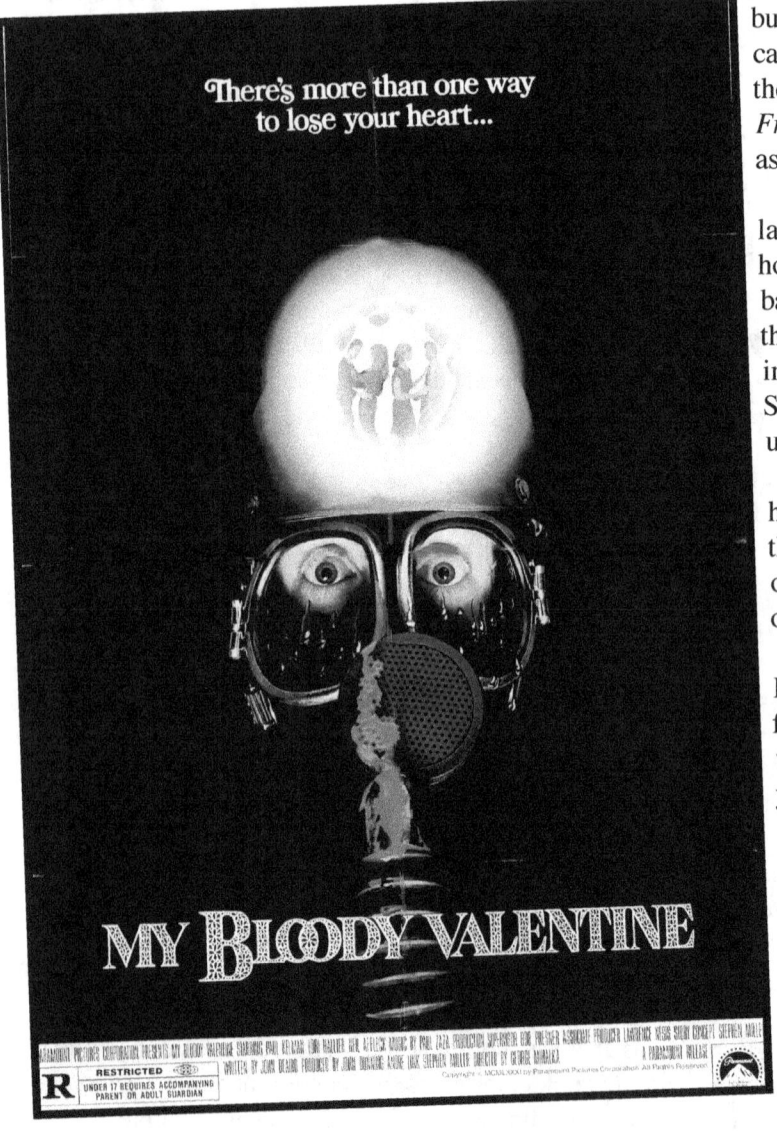

he also laid down the notes for another questionable but seriously effective Can-Con hack-'em-up I loved called *My Bloody Valentine*. And then I learned that the Pam Grier-starring, pre-*Robocop* cyborg thriller *Frankenstein '88* (aka *The Vindicator*) had his sound as well. This Zaza guy was okay by me...

Cut to my grade nine music class six months later. At that point I was a pimply faced teenager, honking away on my cumbersome and slightly embarrassing alto sax. When our class was informed that a gentleman named "Mr. Zaza" was coming in as a guest instructor, I flipped. Could it be the SAME Mr. Zaza whose violent soundscapes in the ultra-tense slasher *Curtains* curdled my blood?

I wasn't far off. As it turned out, it was actually his father, a man who was very amused to learn that a youngster such as me was tripping over his own tongue lavishing praise upon his semi-famous offspring.

But back to this lunch thing. The Bloor Street Diner. Me, Paul Zaza, burgers and Frites (not fries, frites). Looking like a less-British Bryan Ferry by way of a *Heat*-era Al Pacino, Zaza belies his 55 years. He's relaxed, handsome and looks at you with bratty brown eyes that mirror his upbeat view of the world and of an industry that has been very kind to him. Between shakes of a stubborn ketchup bottle, I manage to begin at the beginning, asking him how he managed to stumble into a life making music for movies.

Not surprisingly, Zaza was a child prodigy, and the official story, or at least the story that evolved over 50 years of re-telling, is the stuff of family legend. Zaza Sr. was a noted jazz musician and he knew talent when he heard it. In his four-year-old son Paul, he heard it in spades. The boy had the bug, picking up any instrument he could find, hammering out little piano melodies and was intensely musical in every aspect of his young life. With pride in his eyes, Dad dragged his lad to Toronto's Royal Conservatory of Music to meet Dr. Dolin, a much-respected professor, who all but laughed in the old man's beaming face. The idea that a four-year-old was some class of musical genius was absurd and how dare he drag the boy into his office demanding to be heard, it was unthinkable. But, being reluctantly curious, Dolin did take some time to pacify the old man and gave Paul a simple pitch test.

"I'm going to play you TWO notes, Paul," the mildly annoyed doctor of music said.

"Turn your back to the piano. You're going tell me which one is higher: the first note I play or the second note I play."

Sizing the request up, the lad allegedly replied, "Well the first note is a C sharp and the second is an E flat and the E flat is higher than the C sharp."

Spiraling around to meet the gaze of the elder Zaza, Dolin said simply, "He starts next Saturday."

The rest as they say, is history.

Zaza stayed at the conservatory under Dolin's tutelage, growing older, wiser, gathering degrees and awards as he went, until the ripe old age of 17 when, feeling his oats, Paul left to become what he became. Almost immediately, he landed a gig at the Royal Alexandra Theatre as a bass player for the rock musical *Hair*. He was living at home rent-free, making a truckload of bread, had the best sports car on his block and, by 18, had financed and constructed his own recording studio.

One rainy Saturday afternoon, Paul got a call from a representative of the band The Fifth Dimension. Apparently they were in town for a sold out show at the CNE Grandstand, their own bass player had taken sick, and since almost every one of their hits were culled from the *Hair* soundtrack, somebody suggested that Zaza might just be their man.

So here was this skinny white kid from the mean streets of Rosedale, wealthy, a working musician, the envy of all the boys on the block, hauling his boney butt on stage with a bunch of funkytown soul brothers in front of thousands of screaming, presumably stoned fans. Could it get any better? As a matter of fact, yes, it could. Turns out the regular bass player's illness evolved into him not coming back at all. And with the abrupt exit, and the 5th Dimension having a big gig in Baltimore the next night, they wanted Paul.

Baltimore led to Dallas, Dallas led to L.A. and L.A. led to a month-long tour. Paul had to put high school on hold for a life of limos and ladies and living large in general. But he was a good Catholic boy and claims that he generally played by the rules, a claim that I accept with slitted eyes and a smirk.

Fast forward to 1971. Paul was married to his high school sweetheart and running a marginally successful recording studio. One afternoon, he was approached by a director from the National Film Board of Canada who had just made a short film about cranes...the birds, not the machines—and simply wasn't happy with the score. Zaza hadn't done any film work, in fact had no previous interest in scoring films, but knew a good gig when he saw one. Summoning the bullshit artist within, he managed to convince the filmmaker that he was an old pro at scoring movies and in fact knew EXACTLY how to save the picture. The director asked to hear some of Zaza's previous soundtrack work, of which he of course had none. However, some months prior, a composer HAD come in and recorded a score that he wrote for a small studio film (which we've been asked not to name). Paul had the film reel in his library, took it out of the box and pawned it off as his own. The director was duly impressed, Zaza got the job and, again, the rest is history.

The chain reacted in kind. One lazy Saturday morning Paul and his wife were watching a typically half-assed show on Hamilton's CHCH TV called *The Lively Woman*. The thing was loaded with music—shitty music at that—and Paul was appalled.

"Who the fuck would write such fucking garbage!" Zaza screamed, incensed at the degree of sonic ineptitude on display. The hot-tempered young musician picked up the phone book and found the producer of the program, a one Lionel Shenken, and, that Monday morning, he got the guy on the horn.

"My name is Paul Zaza," he said.

"You don't know me, but I'm a film composer. Tell me...do you produce a show called *The Lively Woman*?"

"Yes, I do," answered Shenken.

Thinking that the WORST Shenken could do was tell him where to go and slam the phone down, Zaza continued in his tirade.

ZAZA: Yeah, well, the music on that show is such shit. It doesn't work.

SHENKEN: Okay...and can you do better?

ZAZA: Not only can I do it better, but I can do it cheaper. You got that music out of a stock library didn't you?

SHENKEN: Yes. As a matter of fact I did.

ZAZA: Well, I'll tell you what I'll do. Not only will I write better music for you, but if you don't like it, you don't have to pay me a cent. So there's really no risk for you is there?

Surprisingly, Shenken did not slam the phone down, but rather invited the fiery lad out to lunch. Zaza ended up composing virtually every show that Shenken produced for the next 20 years. They made millions of dollars together and became close friends.

"You have to have balls…BIG balls if you're going to make it in this business," Zaza tells me between sips of Perrier.

During the '70s Paul built a resume. He went to parties and made contacts. He began to dabble in features; questionable no-budget tax shelter turkey's like *You'll Never Miss It* and the serviceable grifter drama *Three Card Monte*. But in 1979, things changed. Paul was introduced to Florida-based film composer Carl Zittrer through Toronto music producer Chris Stone. Zittrer was the artist famous for working with minor genre legend Bob Clark, the Louisiana native who had developed a cult as a result of such schlocky gems like 1972's *Children Shouldn't Play With Dead Things*, the skin crawling *Deathdream* and the trendsetting 1974 Canadian stalk 'n' stab classic *Black Christmas*.

Zittrer had been commissioned to score the latest Canadian-financed Clark project, *Murder by Decree*, a relatively huge-budgeted Gothic mystery thriller that pit Christopher Plummer's Sherlock Holmes and James Mason's Dr. Watson against the bloody rampage of Jack the Ripper. The film was to be shot on location in London, England and the producers required a full symphonic score. Zittrer was in over his head and he knew it, so he contacted Stone to outsource someone who could assist in arranging, composing and conducting the complex piece of work. That man was Paul Zaza.

With his wife and newly minted infant son in tow, Paul made the trip to jolly old England for what was to be one of the defining gigs of his serpentine career, one in which the fledgling composer would actually find himself conducting The London Symphony Orchestra.

Bob Clark was a visionary, a bit insane but a stylist with a knack for dark imagery and *Murder by Decree* was something of a fog-drenched masterpiece, hailed in some circles as the finest Holmes film ever made and the basis for the Alan Moore-penned graphic novel *From Hell*. Unfortunately, Clark all but demolished his reputation as a master of horror three years later with the hugely successful, utterly deplorable T&A teen flick *Porky's*. By then, Zaza and Clark had become friends, and Clark, being loyal, liked to work with his friends. Zaza and Zittrer would follow Clark through two *Porky's* movies and the holiday favorite *A Christmas Story* before Zaza returned, solo, for Clark's Timothy Hutton graffiti terrorist melodrama *Turk 182*. The two would also tackle A-list features like the quirky Judd Nelson vehicle *From the Hip* and the hideous talking infant comedies *Baby Geniuses* and *Baby Geniuses 2*.

"I spoke to Bob yesterday," Paul told me.

"He's been approached to do a *Black Christmas* remake, but he's tired of the business, I think. Worn out, run down. I mean Christ, he's almost 60, he's getting on…Hell, aren't we all!"

Several months after our lunch, a drunk driver in L.A. killed Bob Clark and his son Ariel. The *Black Christmas* remake was made with Clark sitting in as executive producer, his final film credit.

• • • • •

In 1980, Zaza and his now partner in sonic crime, Carl Zittrer, got a call from the Simpson brothers, a brood of street smart, feudal, film producing siblings from Glasgow. The Simpsons invited them to see a rough cut of a new picture they had been working on, a slasher film in the vein of John Carpenter's hugely popular *Halloween*. The film in question was to become the pounding cinematic tax-dodge migraine that became known as *Prom Night*.

The original version of this tacky cut 'em up classic was even more a chore to sit through than the one we know today. Sitting in a darkened theatre with the burly Simpson boys for the first time, Zaza witnessed one of the lamest excuses for a horror film he'd ever seen. Needless to say, come the 90-minute mark, the brothers weren't digging it either and eventually David Simpson bolted up red-faced and turned to the others in the audience bellowing, "Is this fucking thing as bad as I think it is, or is it worse? What the fuck have we made here boys! I think we just blew a million bucks! We gotta cut this fucker up for guitar picks!"

Zaza hated it too. It wasn't scary, funny, dramatic or coherent...it was useless on almost every level. Three months later Zaza and Zittrer got a call back to see a new cut of the film. The Simpsons were trying desperately to salvage the picture and they wanted Zaza's input. It was time for the fledgling composer to flex his sense of cinematic style.

Zaza fully understood the relationship between sound and image and how to exploit it for maximum returns. A student of Hitchcock, Paul understood the impact of Bernard Herrmann's music and how over the most seemingly benign of visual, it could transform the mundane into the horrific, seemingly effortlessly. In *Prom Night*, Zaza actually requested that the producers shoot a scene of a telephone and they complied. In the final scene, the camera roams the hallways and across the phone wire, all to the low bow-on cello drags of Paul's music. A voice over hisses the victim's name, "Kelllllly," and bingo—real, unnerving horror is achieved without the aid of special effects, but simply, gracefully, with layers of menacing sound.

Peter Simpson, again, desperate to save his squandered million and a half, brought Paul and Carl into his office.

"You want to score this thing?" the producer asked in his thick Scottish burr. "You got it."

ZAZA: Don't we get a contract?

Simpson immediately whips out a checkbook and cuts a check for $25,000.

"Here's your fucking contract! But I'm warning you... you fuck this up and I'll come after you and I'll fucking kill you!"

Needless to say, the score, even the ultra-funky original disco music that climaxes the picture, is the saving grace of the film. *Prom Night* was finally released near the end or 1980, made 43 million and ushered in the new wave of low-budget Canadian slasher movies that followed. The Simpsons spat out three more *Prom Night* pictures over the next decade and Zaza scored each and every one of them. Thankfully, he was never murdered by the bloodthirsty Scot.

"Peter had balls," Zaza said to me, stone-faced. "And as I said, you gotta have balls to make it in this business."

Simpson was not a director. The film fell apart. It was a barely released mishmash that bombed. But viewed today, it works, due in no small part to Zaza's nightmarish orchestral score.

When the title block appears onscreen, the strings scream and the blood freezes. When the hag-masked killer skates up to lay the deathblow on her figure-eight carving victim, Zaza builds tension to the point of nausea. This is the work of a man who again, understands that music in the horror film isn't just aural lubricant to move the shock forward, but rather a character, as vital to the finished film as the actors, cinematographers and directors themselves, if not more so.

When asked who his favorite composer is, Paul cites the work of Ennio Morricone:

> He has written the most terrifying music for the horror film...no one can come close to him. He has the magic. He can bring new meaning to what you see...he can create horror that is almost beautiful, his mastery of mood...brilliant. He is a true artist. To this day, the finest soundtrack I've ever heard is his work on DePalma's *The Untouchables*. Absolutely stunning.

The day is getting old and Paul's story is almost told. He's still married to his childhood sweetheart, the father of a son (Justin Zaza, who is a successful counter-culture novelist) and two daughters and he's still partially running his King and Dufferin studio. Paul is content in life, save for one thing: work. Granted, he needn't ever work again, due to the royalties he receives and invested wealth, but the Canadian industry is floundering.

I see him sauntering around his mammoth recording space, sitting at his desk and waiting. He needs a challenge, a new kind of kick and the fact that that phone just ain't ringing anymore is a crime in itself. Zaza is our own Herrmann, Morricone, Mozart and Beethoven rolled into one ferociously talented package. Such is the sign of our cinematic times that he isn't worshipped with more fervor.

He pays our lunch bill in cash. He tips well. He straightens his casual black suit and gets in his black SUV. I get in the passenger seat. Offering to drop me off at the local metro, I grit my teeth as Paul zips in and out of rush hour traffic like a four-wheeled, monoxide-belching viper. The man has balls, and you need balls to make it, right, Paul?

But sometimes you need more than industrial strength testicles to make a movie. 1983's *Curtains* was stitched together much the same way *Prom Night* was. The film was again, produced by the Simpsons and this time was directed by Richard Ciupka. But Ciupka ran afoul of Peter Simpson. They hated each other and Simpson eventually fired Ciupka, stepped in, big cojones and all, and tried to finish the film himself. Except the perpetually pissed-off

THE SHOUT
1975

Starring John Hurt, Alan Bates and Susannah York
Written by Robert Graves, Michael Austin and
Jerzy Skolimowski
Directed by Jerzy Skolimowski

Whether it be a low, wet, growl coming from deep within in the dark, a disembodied whisper from behind a long-locked door, or the skin-tightening timbre of a terrified woman's pre-knife-kissing scream, the use of sound has been manipulated since the dawn of horror cinema as a highly effective tool to terrify those lucky enough to blessed with good hearing. Sound fills in the blanks, giving audible life to seemingly benign objects, people and events and in turn transforms them, occasionally rendering them downright shuddery. Sometimes sound is used to create tension, provide the aural punch line to an unbearable set up and sometimes even to lull the viewer into a false sense of calm before unleashing whatever beast the filmmaker has heretofore kept under wraps. But in Polanski pal Jerzy Skolimowski's long lost 1978 shocker *The Shout*, sound is used for even more aggressive purposes…to maim, to harm, to inflict agony and eventually, to kill every living thing in its path.

What's that BSB reader? Never heard of *The Shout*? Trust me friend, you ain't alone. This little-seen masterpiece of arthouse shock has never before been available on DVD on these shores and its Columbia Pictures VHS release is so far out of print it's virtually acid washed. I first encountered *The Shout* the same way I first encountered many a brilliant and obscure unsung genre gem, alone, on late night television and, after it finished its 2 hour run, the tiny bones in my ears were paralyzed and pleading for release. This strange, dark and slowly paced film marked me the deepest and not a day went by that I didn't think about it in some way, shape or form. My admiration for it increased when I realized that basically no one I knew had ever seen it, let alone were aware of its existence and it felt as though it were mine, a secret slice of cinema whose fan club sported one member, me. Imagine my delight when, only last week, sifting through the delete bins at Toronto's Queen Video in The Bloor Street Annex, I found that very same aforementioned discontinued videocassette, lying there, moldy, stanky and battered at the bottom of the barrel, being sold off for the princely sum of one lousy dollar. Money immediately changed hands and within seconds, *The Shout* was mine. I played that tape that very night, slipping it deep within the cozy confines of my archaic, nearly forgotten top loader VCR. It seemed appropriate. (Why is this entry starting to sound like a horror geek's *Letters to Penthouse*?)

But, per usual, I get ahead of myself. Let me make you a little savvier to both the picture's plot and to the many ways in which this film is awesome. Here we go…

Church organist and erstwhile experimental music composer Anthony (the great John Hurt, he of David Lynch's *The Elephant Man* and so many wonderfully eccentric turns) and his comely wife Rachel (the tasty British bird Susannah York) live a quiet, idyllic yet sexually vacant life in the English countryside. Into their pleasant but unremarkable home comes a brooding, ruggedly handsome, hirsute wanderer named Crossley (the late, legendary and notoriously self-destructive British actor Alan Bates) seeking refuge and a hot meal, which the young couple skeptically oblige. It's not long before

John Hurt recoils from Alan Bates's primal scream.

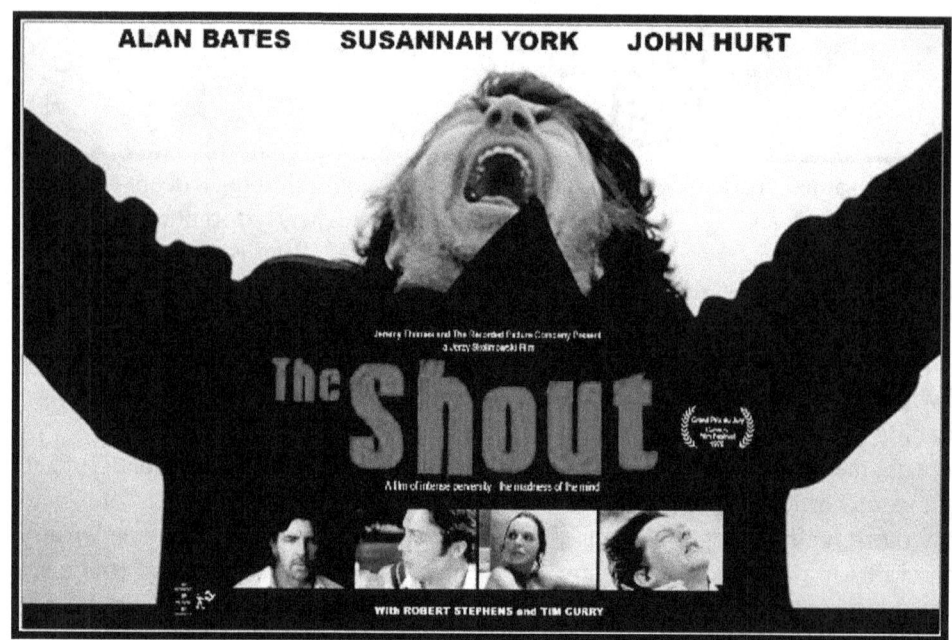

Told as an extended flashback to *Rocky Horror* vet Tim Curry, *The Shout* is the kind of lyrical, intelligent, enigmatic and frustrating work of psychological horror that the Brits were once so very fond of producing in the 1970s and that are simply, and sadly, not being made at all anymore. Filled with deranged, politically incorrect sex (fans of the lovely, mature York take note), haunting nightmare imagery and an aura of icy, inevitable doom, the picture plays like the bastard offspring of *The Wicker Man* (the real one, you ninny, not that horrible Nic Cage thingie...), Nick Roeg's similarly this belligerent, sneering animal of a man begins slowly, methodically manipulating and controlling Anthony and Rachel's lives, both physically and mentally. Turns out Crossley isn't just your run-of-the-mill raving psychotic narcissist, but rather is a kind of an aboriginal warlock, a dangerous outback-dwelling monster who claims to have murdered his children in order to learn the ancient art of psychic vampirism and the ever useful skill of killing by shouting. Taking the disbelieving Anthony onto the moors one night, Crossley crassly proves his case by simply opening his mouth, drawing in air and letting loose a lethal primal shriek from the very chasms of Hell. Things get very nasty and, needless to say, do not end particularly well...

Above: Susannah York under the sheets.
Below: Alan Bates has a scream that puts Munch to shame.

forgotten gem *Don't Look Now* and vintage Luis Bunuel; a movie of surreal, shocking, confusing, terrifying and occasionally downright hilarious power and the kind of eyeball-spinning head-scratcher that stays with you for weeks (in my case, years), requires multiple viewings and asks far more questions than it provides answers to. Driven by a powerful score by Genesis alumni Mike Rutherford and Tony Banks, this is truly a living, breathing nightmare committed to celluloid and I beg, nay command you to seek out a copy, like, yesterday. Do it, or I'll scream.

SOLE SURVIVOR 1983

Starring Anita Skinner, Kurt Johnson, Caren L. Larkey
Written and Directed by Thom Eberhardt

Now, I don't want to be one of those insufferable genre film journalists whose every written word is designed to worm its way onto the theatrical posters or video boxes of even the most half-arsed horror title. That said, I'm really happy that my glowing quote for Thom (*Night of the Comet*) Eberhardt's shuddery 1983 shocker *Sole Survivor* sits squarely upon the top left corner of the back sleeve on Code Red's long overdue 2008 DVD release. See, I'm connected to this film. It means something to me to ensure that every time some lucky stiff sticks the flick into his or her player that they are acutely aware of my undying admiration for it.

But let me back up a bit…

When I was 12, I stayed up late on Halloween night to catch a cable screening of Dan O'Bannon's *The Return of the Living Dead*. And though my mind was suitably blown by that brain-biting classic, it was the feature that followed that truly wound its way around my frantically beating heart. The film in question was indeed Eberhardt's quietly nerve-shredding paean to post-mortem mayhem, *Sole Survivor* and it simply did me in. Leveled me. Total wipeout.

But the next morning, when I went looking for printed references for this impossibly horrifying picture I quickly learned that, outside of the piddly synopsis in the pages of the pay *TV Guide*, no one had seemed to have written a word about it anywhere. Not even good old, pre-internet film book guru Leonard Maltin bothered to include a synopsis. No one I knew had seen it, I had no one to share my enthusiasm with and the ensuing search to obtain a copy of it became a major pre-and post-teenage obsession. Finally, years later when I was entering my 20s, I gripped my mitts on an ancient, coveted out of-print Vestron VHS copy and watching it again confirmed my recollections: That this was the scariest film I'd ever seen…ever. And I mean that.

Sole Survivor casts Chloe Sevigny look-alike Anita Skinner as Denise Watson, the titular single living passenger found amidst the debris of a catastrophic plane crash. After the initial shell shock (and blood spattered nightmares which feature a wide-eyed, gut-leaking torso) subsides, life slowly carries on, save for one rather distressing element: everywhere the poor lass goes, hollow-eyed, slack-jawed, pasty-skinned mute weirdos follow. They stare at her through restaurant windows; they harass her in public parks; they block her way on country roads. They're everywhere, all the time, and alarmingly, their numbers are multiplying. It doesn't take Denise long to

Denise Watson (Anita Skinner) is the sole survivor of a plane crash, but her problems are just beginning.

David Anthony's minimalist ambient score whisper across an empty, rain-slicked city street in the middle of the night, we know that we're about to be plunged into the heart of celluloid darkness. And we are. And it's good.

Sole Survivor is a supremely slow, obscenely eerie exercise in pure, undiluted *Twilight Zone*ish terror that manages to reference Rod Serling, Ingmar Bergman and George Romero, sometimes within the same scene. It's an admittedly depressing picture, one in which realize the truth about her tormenters, that they are the recently risen angry dead whose mission it is to bring her briefly lucky ass back into the black where she belongs.

If this chilling narrative twist sounds familiar, it should. *Sole Survivor* takes its cues from Herk Hervey's immortal low-budget 1962 mood piece *Carnival of Souls* and, by all outward appearances, the more recent *Final Destination* film franchise seems to borrow much from *Sole Survivor*. But what makes Eberhardt's understated shocker superior to both of these considerably more celebrated, reaper-cheating riffs is its straight-faced approach to the fantasy and a relentlessly gloomy, hypnotically somber atmosphere that works symbiotically with really creepy musical accompaniment. From the first frame, when the rumbles of

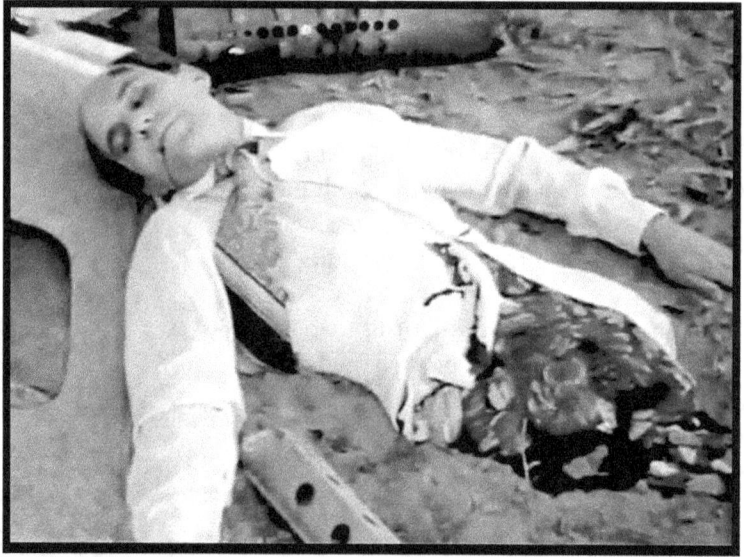

Unfortunately, none of the other passengers were as lucky as Denise.

A friend of Denise meets an untimely end via a swimming pool and a zombie hitman.

we know our heroine is doomed and we can only watch, helpless, as every move she makes just slams another nail in her cosmically preordained coffin. Why Eberhardt has all but disowned it is anyone's guess...

So now you know why that personalized copy of *Sole Survivor* on DVD means so much to me. Now you understand why every review on the internet that now champions this terrifying little film vindicates my sensibilities. And if you value skillfully orchestrated, low-budget American death dreams that seep under your skin and stay there, I advise you to seek this gem out... before it finds *you*.

ACKNOWLEDGEMENTS

Thanks to *Fangoria* for giving me a weekly outlet for my words; to John Cameron, Danielle Ouimet, Harry Kumel, Fabio Frizzi, Mark Damon, Mickey Rourke, Norman J. Warren, Richard Matheson, Amanda Donohoe, Alessandro Alessandroni, Roger Corman, Stephen Rea, Michael Winner, Paul Zaza and Tobe Hooper for lending credibility to the text; to *Rue Morgue* for being my ground zero; to mom and dad for teaching me to love movies and allowing me to stay up late and explore the less sophisticated fare; to Carrie for accepting all the mayhem rather well…

Special thanks to Paulomi Patel for cleaning me up.

And to all of the people who make movies that misbehave.

You continue to inspire.

More to come...

ABOUT THE AUTHOR

Chris Alexander is a Canadian film journalist, radio personality and music composer. He was a critic and columnist with noted horror entertainment periodical *Rue Morgue* for five years before joining the ranks of legendary NYC-based genre magazine *Fangoria*, a publication he and every other oddball kid was obsessed with as a child. He was also the only Canadian critic chosen to box noted "bad filmmaker" Uwe Boll in the "Raging Boll" event in Vancouver, September 2006. He lost brilliantly but not before vomiting a geyser of fake blood at the none-too-amused director.

Chris Alexander lives in Toronto with his wife Carrie and their two sons, Jack and Elliot.

IF YOU ENJOYED THIS BOOK
CALL OR E-MAIL FOR A FREE CATALOG

OR VISIT OUR WEBSITE AT
WWW.MIDMAR.COM

Midnight Marquee Press
9721 Britinay Lane
Baltimore, MD 21234

410-665-1198

www.ingramcontent.com/pod-product-compliance
Lightning Source LLC
Chambersburg PA
CBHW081726100526
44591CB00016B/2522